T0190931

OBJECTLESSONS

A book series about the hidden lives of ordinary things.

Series Editors:

Ian Bogost and Christopher Schaberg

Advisory Board:

In association with

 Georgia Tech | **Center for Media Studies**

BOOKS IN THE SERIES

blanket

KARA THOMPSON

BLOOMSBURY ACADEMIC
NEW YORK • LONDON • OXFORD • NEW DELHI • SYDNEY

BLOOMSBURY ACADEMIC
Bloomsbury Publishing Inc
1385 Broadway, New York, NY 10018, USA
50 Bedford Square, London, WC1B 3DP, UK
29 Earlsfort Terrace, Dublin 2, Ireland

BLOOMSBURY, BLOOMSBURY ACADEMIC and the Diana logo are trademarks of
Bloomsbury Publishing Plc

First published in the United States of America 2019
Reprinted in 2022

Copyright © Kara Thompson, 2019

For legal purposes the Acknowledgments on p. 151 constitute an extension
of this copyright page.

Cover design: Alice Marwick

Names: Thompson, Kara, author.
Title: Blanket / Kara Thompson.
Description: New York, NY : Bloomsbury Academic, [2018] | Series: Object lessons
| Includes bibliographical references and index.
Identifiers: LCCN 2018032988| ISBN 9781628922653 (pbk. : alk. paper) |
ISBN 9781628922653 (paperback) 9781628922677 (epdf)
Subjects: LCSH: Blankets–History. | Blankets–Social aspects. |
Blankets–Psychological aspects.
Classification: LCC TX315 .T46 2018 | DDC 645/.4–dc23 LC record available at
https://lccn.loc.gov/2018032988

ISBN: PB: 978-1-6289-2265-3
ePDF: 978-1-6289-2267-7
eBook: 978-1-6289-2266-0

Series: Object Lessons

Typeset by Deanta Global Publishing Services, Chennai, India
Printed and bound in Great Britain

To find out more about our authors and books visit www.bloomsbury.com
and sign up for our newsletters.

For Kevin

It's all a little touchingly pathetic. To live like this,
a grown creature telling ghost stories,

staring at pictures, paralyzed for hours.

— Max Ritvo, "Dawn of Man"

CONTENTS

A NOTE TO THE READER

I magine a blanket unfolded and tossed onto a chair or bed. Maybe there is no need to imagine, but only to look up from this page and see it for yourself. Was it disregard or a lack of time that created the rumpled and unruly mass? Or is the unfolded blanket a promise to return?

To unfold a blanket, to prepare for cover, is to anticipate a feeling: perhaps most commonly, of warmth, security, or rest. But sometimes, to unfold a blanket is to bask in grief, or to feel absence. To unfold means to reveal and disclose, or to develop and progress, as in *the events unfolded*. To unfold might be to discover something new as it occurs in real time (even if *real time* is itself an illusion, a sleight of hand that objects pull on the human brain), or to lay bare—to make open and exposed what has long been secreted and protected by folds within folds. To fold and unfold a blanket is to touch a memory, to access past and future, perhaps from an otherwise banal or forgettable now. Unfolding is not an undoing, but an intimate exchange.

Notes—endnotes and footnotes—often function as sites for an author's sense of play, where another kind of unfolding takes place. The spaces detached and delineated from the main text may offer a shift in tone, or a space for ideas that could not be contained by the body itself. See www.blanketsandfolds.com for more notes, static and moving images, and updated suggestions for further reading.

PREFACE: CONVOLUTE

In a way, this book has always eluded me, a shapeless form tossed into my future which I knew I would one day need to fold into prose. I couldn't grasp its boundaries or its ambitions because a blanket can be *anything*, really, anything that covers and insulates, protects, obscures, or makes one feel secure. Blankets can be made of wool, cotton, pine boughs, skin, another body, snow, smog, fog, rocks, sidewalks, grass, cities. Blankets are everywhere and anything, banal and extraordinary. They are matters of life and death. The human body will perish of hypothermia faster than starvation.

By taking the blanket as object seriously, we come to understand the inescapable paradox it presents: what it covers is that which is most exposed. Blankets cover—as in hide and saturate—histories of imprisonment and incarceration. Blankets also bear the weight of massacre, whose indiscriminate brutality they cannot cover or hide, but rather, bring into the foreground. Photographs of Lakota people killed by the US Cavalry on December 29, 1890, at Wounded Knee in present-day South Dakota illustrate—in the most traumatic ways—that at times there is no clear line between body and blanket, organic and inorganic, alive and dead.

There may be no more intimate object than a blanket. It swaddles and caresses. It provides safety and security. Blankets contain our skin and hair; they're stained with the accidents and mishaps of our lives, our bodies. Those inexplicable holes in a blanket might be the mark of an insect's presence in some past time. Whether they feed on natural fibers or thrive on the substances humans leave behind (food, hair, sweat, and other bodily traces), as the insects eat they cut holes in the fabric and leave their mark. Insects animate the blanket; if we were able to see them feeding on its fibers and traces, we might see the blanket move, its shape and pattern transformed by the critters' labors and pleasures.

To eliminate moths and other insects with toxic substances (like naphthalene and paradichlorobenzene) is to conjure an environment of human-centered delusion, where the messiness of our living lures critters to their annihilation. Our closet ecosystems, the loops in our rugs and the rub of folded blankets host the troubles of our times. As vibrant matter, blankets assemble and absorb lives that are predominantly imperceptible to humans, or at least not always present and available to our perceptions. Sheep, silkworms, moths, beetles, stars, stories, hands, hair, and fluids make and animate blankets. So do viruses.

Seemingly innocuous and forgettable, discarded in seats or on the floor as passengers shuffle down the aisle and off the plane, airline blankets are carriers of microbes and emblems of micro-capital flows. The World Health Organization's most recent guide to aviation hygiene and sanitation stipulates that blankets should be removed if soiled, but otherwise collected, folded, and re-stowed in overhead bins; during overnight stopovers, blankets should be collected and replaced.[1] A spokesperson for JetBlue explained in 2008 that blankets or pillows could be used for four to six flights before being replaced.[2] That same year, JetBlue started charging for blankets, and other airlines soon followed suit—perhaps motivated less by germs than by an economy of fee-based comfort. In 2016, Delta Airlines introduced the exclusive Westin Heavenly In-Flight blanket for first-class passengers. The "muted grey hue" of the Heavenly Blanket "exudes a relaxing and calming ambiance, while simultaneously paying tribute to the two brands."[3] Westin counts on the hotel consumer not to think of bedbugs or bodily fluids, and Delta on the first-class passenger to sleep soundly under the Heavenly blanket, without thinking *too much* about the afterlife as they travel forty thousand feet above the earth.

Long before I knew I would write a book about blankets, I watched a dear aunt make a bed perfectly, with sheets she had spent some time ironing first. No doubt my grandmother, her mother, taught her that. And while I will never iron my sheets and pillowcases, I think of aunts and grandmas when I take care to place and smooth a fitted sheet—the crucial base that determines the number of wrinkles in succeeding layers. To make a blanket, or even to fold a blanket or wear a blanket, is to make a record. Blankets are objects of inheritance. They keep codes and pass on secrets. This book could be about any number of things, because so too are blankets, and I'm haunted by how different *Blanket* would be if it were written by a different person. I suppose any writer could claim the same anxiety, but still, there's something particularly daunting about the prolific sites of knowledge and forms of inheritance when it comes to the blanket—an object so intimate, so closely associated with generational time.

I wrote much of this book in Los Angeles, and I let the city set my course. Tree roots, displaced cement, smog, skylines, fault lines, traffic, trails, fog, the ocean, and art transformed my sense of blankets and my vision for *Blanket*. I would not have been able to complete this book without Los Angeles, a city covered in fancy and fantasy, full of aspirations. LA is at once grounded, confident, and also fragile, vulnerable. Its current affordable-housing crisis forces more and more people to make their temporary homes on sidewalks and freeway underpasses, where blankets make shelters and beds—where the blanket is a cover for getting by.

I encountered a coyote almost every evening on my walks that summer. Skinny and searching, she made her home at a neighborhood intersection where the road curved uphill. I shouldn't write that I *encountered a coyote on my nightly walk* because really, I went looking for her after I realized seeing her in that spot a few times wasn't a coincidence. This juncture was her home, displaced and unnatural. More than once, I caught drivers stopping to feed her from their cars, as if the neighborhood were a drive-through wildlife park. A few times she followed me. Blankets were always on my mind in LA, especially on those walks; by association, blankets now cleave to the coyote.

I later read about *Ma'ii*, or Coyote, "agent of disorder who arouses the need to keep things in their place at the loom" and in the world for the Diné (Navajo people). Based on their interviews with Diné weavers, Roseann Sandoval Willink and Paul Zolbrod describe Coyote's objections to immorality:

> Everlasting life, he argues, would be deadening. No cornstalk or blade of grass would have to struggle to produce food and keep warm. One season would not follow the next. With perfect immortality, nothing would change. There would be imperfection if there is to be a dynamic, living world, in rugs as well as in a dynamic universe. (4–5)

For Diné weavers, Coyote is not only associated with blankets (or *rugs*, their general term to designate an object of weaving);

he is at the loom. Weaving is a process that incorporates Diné worldviews, stories, ceremonies, colonization: rugs reenact creation, they summon the past and collapse distinctions between past, present, and future (14–15, 19). Weaving is also the product of the weaver's mindset. Diné women weave what they see, and observation is "an ongoing process, not a singular event" (40). In this sense, rugs are also dynamic—women weave what they see, and then other Diné see and communicate with that creation again and again. By seeing the blanket's life, these viewers *encounter* life: a way of seeing, a return, a story, a relative, a past, a future.

But that is not my story, or my inheritance—which is one of the reasons *Blanket* veers from an intimate engagement with Diné weaving. Though this certainly could be a topic in a book nominally *about* blankets, these are stories for Diné to tell. But I can't help but think about the coyote in my neighborhood in LA. We were both transplants. She should have been in Griffith Park's folds, feasting on rabbits and finding companions. I've never had the chance to call LA home, but my fleeting and temporary lives there over the years have always offered me a sense of security, the comfort of being *at home*. And it was only the inhabitance of this feeling that allowed me to finish *Blanket*, which *is* a book about inheritance and stories. *Blanket* tells stories of extraction, codes, covers, viruses, sheep, prison, camp, and death. *Blanket* takes us to minerals and rocks that tell time, like copper and marble; it also takes us to the folds of infinity. This is a project of contingency and magic.

I've called this preface *convolute* because the concept traverses biology, geology, and language—all blanket forms. Convolute describes something rolled into itself, as in a leaf or a flower bud, or a blanket. Convolute is a type of fold, so that what is interior and hidden eventually becomes exposed, exterior—an infinite unfolding. A convolute fold may also refer to a distinct fold in sedimentary rock, which denotes a radical event, a disturbance, a moment in time when everything changed. Convolute is a type of archive, a trace to be encountered in the future. Walter Benjamin organized his fragments and notes into convolutes (*Konvolut* in German means "sheaf" or "bundle")—a style particularly evident in *The Arcades Project*. His paragraphs are assemblages of thought, archives of a fleeting moment that is now, still, with us. The convolute paragraphs form the body of his texts, and as with all bodies, the coherence and coming together can sometimes be messy, even convoluted. Yet somehow it works.

I consider this book a *study*, to borrow a term from art—writing as a mode of preparation for the blanket, or another medium and format to understand the blanket. Blankets are also filaments of language: a *blanket statement*, a *blanket stipulation* in contracts. Or *blankety-blank*: the origin of *blanket*, from Old French, *blankete, blanquette* < *blanc* + *-ette,* the little white, the empty space, the ellipsis or elision. Blankets are metaphors, and they also speak and signify in syntax beyond human discernibility. For me, the blanket is most interesting on the edge of its own materiality, when it threatens to be not completely itself. In *The Art of Death*,

Edwidge Danticat explains that we "write about the dead to make sense of our losses, to become less haunted, to turn ghosts into words, to transform an absence into language" (29). But all language is absence. Words are ghosts. And despite our efforts to *make sense* of loss, we're left with ghosts and metaphors—stored, carried, transmitted, covered, and exposed in blankets.

UNFOLD 1

When I try to write about blankets, I tell a story about death.

1 WITNESS

The full metal jacket bullet is a kind of blanket object: an outer layer made of a copper alloy covers or blankets a softer core, usually made of lead. Because these bullets exit the bodies they penetrate, they create massive internal trauma and then go on to inflict even more damage. Police departments in the United States have increasingly switched to hollow-point bullets because they reduce "collateral damage": These bullets fragment, fracture, and linger inside the first body they hit.[1] But in international armed combat, in keeping with the 1899 Hague Declaration Concerning Expanding Bullets, the US military only activates full metal jackets.

The title of Stanley Kubrick's 1987 film about the Tet Offensive refers to the ammunition soldiers used in the Vietnam War. But *Full Metal Jacket* also contends with the traumas of combat, which are repressed and later expressed in the anxious and tenuous seams between violence and homoeroticism. The first section of the film dramatizes the grueling itineraries of Marines basic training. The scenes focus on the failures of one private against the resilience of another as each endures the inflammatory insults of their drill instructor, Gunnery Sergeant Hartman. Hartman demands that Private James T. Davis, nicknamed "Joker" for his use of irony and sarcasm, must mentor, guide, and even cajole Private Leonard Lawrence, or "Pyle," to complete the physical and mental tasks and tests of basic training. Hartman targets Pyle because of his size, his lack of athleticism, his desire for food, and (what gets portrayed as) his intellectual disability. Joker seems to take up the directive admirably. He exercises a teacher's patience with an air of paternal, even coach-like, intimacy. In one scene, he encourages Pyle to climb a tall structure that resembles an oversized ladder; when Pyle reveals his fear by quietly crying and hesitating to throw his leg over the top bar in order to climb down the other side, Joker waits with him and repeats "Atta boy" and "That's it."

The scene shifts to the two in close proximity, nearly touching: Joker kneels at the head of a bed, and Pyle sits and watches intently as Joker shows him how to create a neat, taut, four-inch fold with blanket and sheet. The next montage confirms that Pyle has learned a great deal—he knows how to position his weapon, he can run and jump onto a rope, he jogs in formation. But after Hartman discovers at bed check that Pyle has hidden a jelly donut inside his footlocker, we sense a distinct shift, a kind of regression, which is made most obvious by infantilizing gestures against Pyle: Hartman commands him to suck his thumb while the others exercise in precise synchrony, and Joker dresses him (buttons his shirt, straightens his collar) while Pyle reveals his anxiety that everyone, including Joker, now "hates" him.

While most of these scenes are brightly lit by sun or overhead fluorescent light, a subsequent shot plunges into low light, a blue cast against a close shot of a white towel. Two hands appear to place a bar of soap on the towel. The hands wrap, twist, and tighten the towel around the soap; the moment concludes with a few strikes of the bed with this newly fashioned weapon. The next shot hovers on Joker in the same blue low light, awake and in bed. He stands up and looks at Pyle, sound asleep in the bunk above his. As all the men climb out of their beds swiftly and stealthily, dressed in identical stark-white boxers and white T-shirts, they amass and multiply like a horde of ghosts. Private Cowboy forces a gag into Pyle's mouth while others cover him with a blanket—an aggressive swaddle. While Pyle is immobilized and unable to scream, the privates beat him with the bars of soap wrapped in towels, striking the blanket and thus his body, one after the other. As the men stream up to the bed to pummel Pyle, their faces morph into grimaces of exertion and exhilaration. Finally Cowboy, working to keep Pyle restrained, yells at Joker to "do it." Joker stands back and strikes Pyle several times in a row with great force, and then slinks into the lower bunk while others remove the blanket and disperse. As Cowboy removes the gag he tells Pyle, "Remember, it's just a bad dream, fat boy," and the scene ends with Pyle's cries of pain, shame, and shock while Joker lies below and covers his ears.

This scene dramatizes a hazing ritual military and fraternity cultures call a "blanket party." While many scenes of trauma follow in *Full Metal Jacket*, the blanket party turns acutely disturbing because it stages the pain and violence in the quiet darkness of bedtime. The weapons and ammunition are domestic, intimate objects: soap, towels, and a blanket. And the one whom Private Lawrence trusts the most, the one who has provided the most care and tenderness, is the one who inflicts the harshest pain. The blanket, towels, and soap—the very objects they could use together in bed or in a shower—come to sanctify their intimacy as violent rather than pleasurable, thus betraying the often indeterminate distinction between the two. *Remember, it's just a bad dream, fat boy* reminds Pyle, and us, that he occupies a different bodily and affective place among them: He's the "fat boy" whose loud cries turn trauma outward, while the others cathect their pain into a bad dream. *Remember* transforms the sentence from a command into a lesson for Pyle's conscious self to repress and cathect, to direct the pain not simply inward but to the unconscious, so that it becomes undetectable as such.

In 1980, five years after the Vietnam War, Post-Traumatic Stress Disorder (PTSD) appeared in the *DSM-III* (Diagnostic and Statistical Manual of Mental Disorders). The official recognition of PTSD as a mental-health condition codified a discourse and diagnosis for the presence and endurance of somatic and psychological forms of trauma that have always accompanied military service and combat.[2] *Trauma* derives from the Greek τραῦμα, meaning *wound*, and initially referred to an external wound or bodily injury. But by the late nineteenth century, psychologists and psychoanalysts used the discourse of trauma to refer to psychic injury, turning attention to the brain itself as the primary organ from which biological and emotional functions originate.[3] Though it is now an outmoded term (and yet still understood to be distinct from PTSD), World War I soldiers and veterans were diagnosed with "shell shock"—the first medicalized description of the imbricated physiological and emotional traumas caused by the technologies of war.[4] The term is at once inescapably literal—the shock associated with the experience of exploding shells or artillery projectile bombs and shrapnel from mortars and grenades, which caused well over half of the 9.7 million military fatalities—and metaphorically rich, particularly if we take into account Freud's speculative text on trauma published in the shadows of World War I.

Beyond the Pleasure Principle (1920) understands trauma as psychic and social, biological and cultural, external and internal. It asks readers to confront what may be counterintuitive: Trauma is a sensation (and even a form of pleasure) we are compelled to repeat precisely because we won't remember the sensation as a site of trauma. And in this compulsion to repeat lies the tension between the conscious and unconscious ego. We seek to avoid the "unpleasure" that would be released if we were to liberate the repressed from the unconscious, but our instincts are compelled by the death drive. The pleasure principle aims, but ultimately fails, to guard against the stimulations from within, the "instincts" that drive us toward death. *Beyond the Pleasure Principle* forwards a theory, which Freud concedes may be difficult to abandon: Humans strive not *forward*, but instead toward an instinct or urge to revert backward, to an "earlier state of things." There is, he argues, an "expression of the inertia inherent in organic life" (43). To illustrate this point, Freud turns to biology and metaphor. He invites readers to "picture a living organism in its most simplified possible form," like a gastropod whose receptive layer, or shell, is turned outward (28). The shell absorbs the pleasures and stimulations of the external world to the point that it ceases to live. That simple organism would not survive the stimulations of the external world without the shell, which it acquires by death: "its outermost surface ceases to have the structure proper to living matter" and to some degree becomes "inorganic and thenceforward functions as a special envelope or membrane resistant to stimuli" (30). Protection against stimuli is almost more important, he maintains, than the reception of stimuli.

The full metal jacket, exploding artillery, and Joker's blanket at once induce trauma and shock by their own material shells—the layers and forms of cover that penetrate a body, a soft target—and yet the shock that causes the psychic and somatic trauma is a result of a compromised shell. *Shock* is the breach of the shell (36). Joker's blanket party exposes the blanket as a site *and* screen for trauma: the object through which their traumas pass, and the object that turns Pyle's pain and sensation outward. The blanket functions as a shell that both protects from *and* produces shock. Pain and pleasure commingle in the blanket's fibers. All "forms of sensation carry with them the trace of trauma. Every organism or body is by definition 'sensitive,' requiring some form of protection from the incursions of the outside world," Ann Cvetkovich explains (53). Stimulation threatens, even if we seek and repeat it. To take the pleasure principle seriously is to understand that pleasure and its analogs (stimulation, penetration) marshal their apparent counterparts, pain and death, so that the body measures and modulates pleasure and unpleasure in order to survive.

Freud's account of trauma and the death drive constructs a discourse of animacy: The shell or protective layer—once *alive*—hardens and eventually dies as it absorbs stimulations, so that even organic bodies live on the threshold between life and nonlife. The scaly-foot snail could be the wish fulfillment of Freud's early twentieth-century speculations. These gastropods survive repeated crab attacks with their ingenious triple-layer blanket: under the outer shell, which they fabricate into iron with the help of bacteria and extreme heat produced from hydrothermal vents in the Indian Ocean, lies a thick but compliant middle layer followed by a strong, calcified interior. A recent study of scaly-foot snails, funded partially by the Department of Defense and led by Christine Ortiz, an associate professor of materials science and engineering at MIT, may help improve armor and other forms of cover for soldiers, police, and first responders— their shells, a medium on the verge of life and death, may serve as a prototype to protect humans from the penetration of bullets like the full metal jacket.[5] The shell, the cover, and the blanket linger in elastic animacy.

When people die in their attempts to summit Mt. Everest, their bodies must be left where they lay. To climb Mt. Everest is to witness a terrain as an archive of death. Survivors cover the bodies with rocks, packs, or national flags in an attempt to mark their passing and hide them from view—blankets as witness marks and memorial covers. When blankets cover dead bodies, the viewer understands this is a body not embalmed for public display, but which nevertheless lies in public view—the result of an unexpected disaster or act of violence, a flash flood, a shooting, the detonation of a bomb. Since we know what's underneath, what does the blanket conceal? Sometimes traces of life soak through. The blanket might relent to the body's shape. What does it feel like to cover a body, one frozen in gestures of surprise or surrender? What does it feel like to be a blanket?[6]

Jane Bennett argues that something constructive "happens to the concept of agency once nonhuman beings are figured less as social constructions and more as actors, and once humans themselves are assessed not as autonomous but as vital materialities" (21). One never acts alone, but always in collaboration with other bodies and forces, what Bennett calls an *agentic assemblage*. A collaboration between blanket and human likely activated the agency of the variola virus, or smallpox, in the eighteenth and nineteenth centuries in order to kill or subdue Native peoples and nations who attempted to protect their homelands through both armed conflict and diplomacy. Variola infects most productively by way of the respiratory tract, by prolonged face-to-face contact. But it can live longer in scabs than in respiratory fluids, and the earliest attempts to inoculate a person infected with the virus used dried smallpox scabs stored and transported on scraps of paper, on threads, or in vases (Mayor 73, no. 7–8). While the veracity and verifiability of the "small-pox blanket" as a weapon of biological warfare have been repeatedly called into question, there is no doubt that blankets and other textiles can host the virus for a prolonged period. And British troops and settlers certainly understood the function of the blanket as trade currency and an agent of survival for Native peoples.

The Seven Years' War ended officially in February 1763, after nine years of conflict for North American territory between Great Britain and France and their respective Native ally nations. But peace was elusive: Britain had seized a vast land space over which it had little to no control, and it was deeply in debt from nearly a decade of war. Its attempts to contend with both its financial crisis and its reach of power eventually led to the American Revolution. But alongside Great Britain's conflicts with American settlers, British troops and colonial militias now fought Native nations who tried to protect their homelands and lifeways. From 1763 to 1766, Chief Pontiac (Ottawa) led a united delegation of Native nations, including Ottawa, Ojibwe, Potawatomi, Huron, Miami (Weas and Piankashaws), Kickapoo, Mascouten, Lenape, Shawnee, Wyandot, Seneca, and Seneca-Cayuga, against British attacks and incursions.

By 1764, Henry Bouquet assumed the role of British commander at Fort Pitt (in present-day Pittsburgh). His correspondence with Lord Jeffery Amherst about Fort Pitt and what Francis Parkman called in 1851 "the formidable nature of the Indian outbreak" reveals a concerted plot to enact biological warfare on Pontiac's delegation. Amherst wrote to Bouquet: "Could it not be contrived to send the small pox among those disaffected tribes of Indians? We must on this occasion use every stratagem in our power to reduce them" (39).[7] In his response, Bouquet lamented that they could not simply "hunt them [Native peoples] with English dogs, supported by rangers and some light horse, who would, I think, effectually extirpate or remove that vermin." Amherst responded, "You will do well to try to inoculate the Indians by means of blankets, as well as to try every other method that can serve to extirpate this execrable race" (40).[8]

Trader and land speculator William Trent recorded in his journal that as two Delaware Indians left Fort Pitt after meeting with British soldiers, they were given blankets infested with smallpox. "Out of regard for them," the soldiers gifted "two Blankets and an Handkerchief out of the Small Pox Hospital." Trent added, "I hope it will have the desired effect."[9] *Out of regard for them* presents the British as benevolent protectors—when in fact they had just gambled on the blankets infecting recipients with smallpox. A smallpox epidemic spread among the southeastern Ohio peoples from 1763 to 1764. The contagion also affected the Ohio Iroquois and Shawnees and further south, the Choctaws, Chickasaws, and Muscogees. During the first four centuries of European colonization, up to 90 percent of Indigenous peoples in the Americas died from viruses such as smallpox, measles, and influenza (Ostler).[10]

Parkman notes that no hard evidence indicates that Bouquet carried out this plan, but a smallpox outbreak indeed devastated Native peoples in the Great Lakes region and Ohio Valley a few months after this correspondence.[11] When those who accepted blankets opened them to wrap the warm fabric around their bodies, they would have inhaled traces of skin and pustule remnants from the blanket's fibers. Once a body was infected with smallpox, the illness could last over five weeks, if the victim survived that long.

In the agential assemblage of British commanders, land speculators and settlers, viruses and disease, blankets, and smallpox, millions of Native people died after European invasion. What should constitute "evidence" and archive when we already know this devastating fact to be true? When does the scenario of the "smallpox blanket"—as a trope, a carrier, a weapon—turn implausible? That the virus lives on a blanket? That the blanket could transfer its agencies from security and warmth to illness and death? That colonial troops sought to defeat Native peoples at any cost in order to steal and settle land? Amherst and Bouquet equated Native people to pests and vermin that needed to be exterminated. Their correspondence does not betray the irony that in their efforts to represent Native peoples as a pestilent species,

European colonization, trade, and practices of enslavement were the very sources of disease and the introduction of rats, cockroaches, and other pests to North America. The blanket provides a cover, but it cannot conceal. For those who dispute these histories, blankets are carriers of rumor and story. But blankets communicate realities that many wish to remain incommunicable.

Smallpox was virtually eradicated in 1980; the remaining traces live in labs. But by 1981, doctors in the United States began to document the prevalence of pneumonia and Kaposi's Sarcoma, a rare type of skin cancer, among gay men in New York and California.[12] By the end of 1981, 121 people were known to have died from these conditions. The following year, the Centers for Disease Control and Prevention determined the cases were related to an immune system disorder they called Acquired Immune Deficiency Syndrome. President Reagan did not publicly utter the word "AIDS" until 1987, and then only to insinuate that it exacts punishment on those who have behaved immorally: "When it comes to preventing AIDS, don't medicine and morality teach the same lessons?"[13]

By the 1993 March on Washington for Lesbian, Gay, and Bi Equal Rights and Liberation, over 440,000 cases of AIDS had been reported; over 270,000 had already died from AIDS or another HIV-related illness. The annual rate of death attributed to HIV infection peaked in 1995. On April 28, 1993, a crewmember on an American Airlines flight from Washington, DC, to Dallas–Fort Worth radioed ahead to request a change of blankets; the ground crew receiving the message transcribed it as "inbd crew req complete chg of all pillows blankets due gay rights activists group onbd." Some of the passengers on this flight had recently attended the March on Washington, and they had likely gazed at large-scale panels from The NAMES Project AIDS Memorial Quilt that covered the National Mall during the march. These twelve-foot-square quilt blocks suture three-foot-by-six-foot handmade quilt panels, each one a memorial to a life overcome by the virus. The panels are covered with names and hieroglyphics of friends, lovers, children, parents, and even philosophers. (Michel Foucault appears on blocks 00076, 00180, 01564, and 04233.) The NAMES Project is a traveling act of mourning and memory, a testimony to trauma. The blanket relies on a cultural nostalgia that not only binds the mourner to the dead, but the mourner and the dead to a history of quilting, an inherited cultural practice and an often-inherited object. The message to the American Airlines ground crew suggested—quite erroneously—that HIV could be transmitted from blanket to flesh; it also presumed an inextricable relation between the virus and the "gay rights activists group onbd."

The blanket covered the National Mall; it also covers a body during a long flight, or a body lying in a hospital bed. But a blanket can also acquire a life other than itself. We may take the blanket for granted as an object, quiet and inert. But when it becomes soiled, whether with food (American Airlines later alleged that the blankets actually needed replacement due to spilled tomato sauce), bodily fluids, or perhaps even a virus, it acquires a kind of vitality. Perhaps what threatened the American Airlines employee who linked *blankets* and *AIDS* was a disjunction wherein this domestic object opened itself to a virtual reality, a kind of viral potential to assemble and replicate, to infect. That is to say, the blanket lives as a virus lives: it occupies some other animate state.

Though HIV is communicable, a barrier such as a latex glove or a condom can interrupt its transmission. On the practice of barebacking, or intentionally having sex without a condom, Tim Dean asks, "What would it mean for a young gay man today to be able to trace his virus back to, say, Michel Foucault?" (89) By way of a risky sexual practice, Dean imagines Foucault might live on. This is Foucault's presence in a body, rather than under a blanket or on a memorial quilt. Barebacking refuses the cover of the condom; it never forecloses the potential for a communicable virus. It beckons the virus, rather than camouflaging it in a quilt or obstructing it with latex. But like the virus, the blanket is also risk and potential. The blanket goes viral when it threatens the security or sentiments of a flight crew, or when it uncovers the subject of HIV/AIDS in a small Midwestern town. A blanket has the potential to communicate homophobia, or a will to colonize and eradicate. Even a blanket covering a body conceals one surface only to expose the blanket itself. In the act of covering up, the blanket betrays itself as an agent of communicable disease, a conveyor of rumor and fear.

FIGURE 1 *Deep Down, I Don't Believe in Hymns* (2001) by Dario Robleto.

In his 2001 installation *Deep Down, I Don't Believe in Hymns*, conceptual artist Dario Robleto turns a blanket back on itself. He infests a military-issued blanket from 1862 with vinyl record dust, specifically the particles of two songs: Neil Young and Crazy Horse's "Cortez the Killer" and Soft Cell's cover of "Tainted Love." "Cortez the Killer" imagines the colonizer with galleons and guns, "dancing across the water" looking for the new world, while Montezuma basks on shore, surrounded by abundance: cocoa leaves, pearls, gold, beautiful women, strong men, and secrets. Although the title critiques "discovery" and conquest, Young cannot resist falling back on the very colonial tropes he wishes to send up. "Cortez [was] the killer"—but the song also hails the beautiful Natives, and a beautiful Native woman, specifically, "who still loves me to this day." The song is infected with tainted love. Robleto makes the infestation visible: up close, one can see that the blanket is covered in ash-like, tiny black specks. The conceptual joke of it all—that a blanket which has been a matter of life and a gift of death is itself now infected with a "tainted love"—depends upon the history and reputation of the smallpox blanket. *Deep Down, I Don't Believe in Hymns* riffs on the blanket's viral capacities, or the ways that the cover mutates, remixes, and finds another host.

The blanket is an intimate witness to histories of settler colonialism in North America. Settler colonials used terms and phrases such as *back to the blanket* and *blanket Indian* as signifiers of regression and primitivity. The degree to which someone had gone "back to the blanket" measured their slipping backward in time, away from the so-called "progress" of settler-colonial civility. *Blanket Indian* could be found in a number of discursive forms, from Commissioner of Indian Affairs reports to popular literature and periodicals.[14] Boarding schools were key disciplinary sites for settler colonials to turn Native children away from the "blanket"—both literally, by taking their blankets and clothes away, and also metaphorically, for blankets were signifiers of lifeways and cultural practices. Once blankets were taken away, Native children were disciplined into a curriculum of hygiene, heteronormativity, and morality. For instance, Estelle Reel's *The Uniform Course of Study for the Indian Schools of the United States* for the Office of Indian Affairs outlines a "housekeeping" regimen: "The good housekeeper is the arbiter of the health of the occupants of the home, and special stress must be laid upon the hygienic and sanitary laws." The good housekeeper also pays attention to "the manners and morals of the members of the family" (148).[15] Reel determines that girls are responsible for making beds in the "method employed in the army," a style that calls to mind the scene of Private Joker teaching Private Pyle in *Full Metal Jacket* (154). Blankets were to be washed on clear, windy days and shaken well beforehand. Soiled spots should be rubbed out with a brush and soap.

Captain Richard Henry Pratt, founder and superintendent of the Carlisle Indian Industrial School in Pennsylvania, used the term *blanket Indians* in multiple contexts and publications, including a conversation with a guest at the Carlisle graduation ceremony in 1896. Pratt delights in the Native commencement speaker's gifts for oration, and then relates this same student's initial resistance to Carlisle. Pratt boasts that he managed effectively to imprison the student long enough in order to turn him from a "blanket Indian" into an "accomplished gentlemen." With tears in his eyes— presumably of pride—Pratt explains, "When that boy first came . . . he declared that he would not stay! Twice he ran away and I went after him and brought him back. I had even to lock him in the guard-house" ("Imprisoned" 434). Pratt's delight marks the co-productions of school and prison disciplinary regimes—a point made crystalline by Pratt's own history as the warden of Fort Marion, a prison in St. Augustine, Florida, to incarcerate Native people, predominantly from the Great Plains and Southwest, who resisted settler-colonial tactics and expropriations.[16] Kiowa, Cheyenne, Arapaho, Comanche, and Caddo prisoners were transported by train from Fort Sill in Oklahoma to Fort Marion, where they appeared "clad only in their blankets, chained hand and foot" (Pratt 181).

Writers such as Zitkala-Ša and Luther Standing Bear claimed the trope of going back to the blanket as one not of regression, but of resurgence and survival. Zitkala-Ša (Dakota) acknowledges the presence and security of her blanket as she's being courted and coerced by missionaries to travel east for school. Education in missionary and boarding schools, her mother reasons, is a kind of "tardy justice" that white settlers offer as payment on their "large debt for stolen lands." Nevertheless, she concludes that her daughter will need to suffer this "experiment" to contend with a future of "fewer real Dakotas." On the day the missionaries come to take Zitkala-Ša by carriage to the train that will take her east, her blanket screens her ensuing trauma. "Wrapped in my heavy blanket, I walked with my mother to the carriage that was soon to take us to the iron horse." She proceeds with a certain measure of happiness and anticipation, especially as she meets up with playmates "who were also wearing their best thick blankets." But as the "white man's horses" swiftly take them away, and her mother becomes a vanishing point, regret takes hold. "I no longer felt free to be myself, or to voice my own feelings. The tears trickled down my cheeks, and I buried my face in the folds of my blanket" (86). Zitkala-Ša's identification with her blanket shifts the ideological pulse of the "blanket Indian" and "going back to the blanket"—the blanket's folds provide security, and a sense of home.

In Luther Standing Bear's (Lakota) *Land of the Spotted Eagle* (1933), he describes the blanket as a kind of shield or guard against settler colonialism: "According to the white man, the Indian, choosing to return to his tribal manners and dress, 'goes back to the blanket.'" However, he adds, "'going back to the blanket' is the factor that saved him from, or at least stayed, his final destruction. Had the Indian been as completely subdued in spirit as he was in body he would have perished within the century of his subjection" (189–91). For Standing Bear, the blanket is a synonym of survivance, a way of refusing the "white man's ways." The blanket, worn "with the significance of language," "covers one of the bravest attempts ever made by man on this continent to rise to heights of true humanity" (191). Signifying what he calls "the prototype of the American Indian," the blanket communicates an act of bravery, given the virality of settler colonialism. Standing Bear's statement also suggests that authenticity—to wear the sign of one's identity—is also a kind of "humanity" not exercised on this continent. The blanket thus communicates a profound critique of settler subjectivity, for the blanket would only need to signify indigeneity if confronted by the threat of its uncovering and removal.

Blankets were a matter of life on the Plains, the homelands of the Oceti Sakowin: the Dakota and Lakota, the Oyates of Zitkala-Ša and Luther Standing Bear, many of whom ended up imprisoned in boarding school or at Fort Marion. Blankets communicate lifeways and traditions; they signify honor and passage. Without them, people died, especially after settlers nearly exterminated the American bison and thus the shelter, warmth, food, economies, and practices the bison provided. And so blankets also communicate the dispossession of lands, and the desperate conditions of dependency in the form of annuities, traders, and Indian Agencies that white settlers conditioned. Blankets witness massacres. And resurgence.

The Ghost Dance movement of the late nineteenth century and its forms of ritual were believed to bring the dead back to life. Kicking Bear (Mniconjou from Cheyenne River) brought the Ghost Dance to the Great Plains from the prophet Wovoka (Paiute) in present-day Nevada. Short Bull brought it to the Rosebud reservation, and others introduced it to Pine Ridge (Brown 508). Chief Sitting Bull at Standing Rock had no objections to people engaging in the Ghost Dance, but he also knew that Indian agents were sending soldiers to stop the ceremonies. The Indian agent at Standing Rock, James McLaughlin, suggested that a "more pernicious system of religion could not have been offered to a people who stood on the threshold of civilization" (qtd. in Brown 510). McLaughlin eventually had Kicking Bear removed from the reservation.

In November 1890, the Office of Indian Affairs in Washington, DC, ordered Indian agents to telegraph the names of Ghost Dancers. Sitting Bull's name was among them. On December 15, Ghost Dancers surrounded his cabin and outnumbered the forty-three police who came to arrest him. Among them was Catch-the-Bear, who confronted Lieutenant Bull Head as he led Sitting Bull to his horse. Catch-the-Bear allegedly threw off his blanket, pulled out a rifle, and fired at Bull Head. Wounded, Bull Head tried to fire back at Catch-the-Bear but missed him and hit Sitting Bull instead. Sitting Bull died from his wounds.

After Sitting Bull's death, Hunkpapas and Mniconjous left Cheyenne River and Standing Rock to seek refuge in a Ghost Dance camp led by Chief Red Cloud at Pine Ridge. Some of them reached Chief Spotted Elk's (Big Foot's) camp near Cherry Creek by December 17, and that same day, the War Department issued orders to arrest Spotted Elk. He had been trying to move his people to Pine Ridge after he learned of Sitting Bull's murder, but in the process, he caught pneumonia and started to hemorrhage. On December 28, as they neared Porcupine Creek, some of Spotted Elk's people sighted the Seventh Cavalry. Covered in blankets and traveling in a wagon because of his poor health, Spotted Elk ordered a white flag to be cast. His blankets were already stained with blood from his pneumonia. Spotted Elk agreed to keep moving toward Wounded Knee Creek the following day. That evening, the soldiers aimed their Hotchkiss guns on the rise overlooking the camp, and in the morning, they ordered the 120 men and 230 women to turn in all weapons, then stripped them of their guns, knives, and ritual belongings (Brown 521).

Donald Blue Hair, a survivor of the Wounded Knee Massacre, later recounted through an interpreter:

> I was with Big Foot's band. The morning after we made our camps there, all of the men were requested to come to the center then they began to search for arms, throwing our blankets back and searching us. They took everything, any kind of knife, even beading awls. (McGregor 117)

Reports from the soldiers indicate that someone refused to be searched and shot his gun, which set off a flurry of bullets from the Army. But all survivors report that a soldier fired his gun as if a signal for battle, *after* all guns and weapons were taken away from the now-prisoners in Spotted Elk's camp. Within minutes, Chief Spotted Elk was dead, still wrapped in his blankets. Survivors describe how soldiers pursued them and shot people as they were trying to surrender. Annie Iron Lavatta or Hakiktawin's 1934 testimony describes the acceleration of the violence, which culminates under the cover of a blanket:

> I was running away from the place and followed those were running away, with my grandfather, and grandmother, and brother, were killed as we crossed the ravine or creek, going up the grade, and then I was shot on the right hip clear through and on my right wrist where I did not go any further as I was not able to walk, and after the soldier picked me up where a little girl came to me and crawled into the blanket. (131)[17]

The cavalry killed over 300 Mniconjou and Hunkpapa Lakota people that morning. Photos taken by US officials days after the massacre, after a blizzard passed over, betray multiple forms of cover. Bodies caught in frozen gestures of surprise and surrender lay on their homelands, some covered in blankets and others piled into mass graves full of blankets and bodies.

In 1973, American Indian Movement (AIM) activists occupied Wounded Knee for seventy-one days to defend treaty rights and homelands. Violence and precarity accelerated and intensified on Pine Ridge between 1973 and 1975, as the US government and tribal council led by Chairman Dick Wilson sought to subdue the energies and commitments of AIM activism. When two FBI agents in unmarked cars and civilian clothing entered the Jumping Bull ranch compound where AIM members were camped, gunfire was exchanged, and both agents were killed. Leonard Peltier (Anishinaabe-Lakota) was later arrested in Canada, extradited to the United States, and tried in a North Dakota court for murder. The federal government's case against him rested on a bullet shell recovered from one of the agents' trunks. Although ballistic tests proved the bullet did not come from Peltier's AR-15, he was convicted and ordered to serve two consecutive life sentences. Despite multiple attempts for clemency, he is still in prison for a crime he did not commit, for a gun he did not shoot, and for bullets in two FBI agents he did not activate.[18]

Every year since 1986, descendants of those massacred at Wounded Knee in 1890 recreate Spotted Elk's journey by horseback from the Standing Rock Sioux Nation's reservation to Wounded Knee. Riders begin the 191-mile trip in mid-December, often in snow, freezing conditions, and blizzards (as were the conditions for Spotted Elk and his people) to arrive at Wounded Knee on the Pine Ridge Indian Reservation by December 29. The inaugural ride took place eleven years after Leonard Peltier was arrested.

Nick Estes' (Kul Wicasa Sicangu Tintonwan) essay "Fighting for Our Lives" foregrounds the accumulations of resurgence that emanate from and resonate between Wounded Knee and Standing Rock. The 1973 occupation "was a culmination of more than a decade of Red Power organizing," and it provided a "catalyst for a mass gathering of thousands at Standing Rock in 1974 . . . ." That gathering of more than ninety Native nations conditioned the founding of the International Indian Treaty Council, which "built the foundations of what would become four decades of work at the United Nations and the basis for the 2007 Declaration on the Rights of Indigenous Peoples," Estes explains. Native scholars and activists, descendants of those who died at Wounded Knee, of Sitting Bull and Red Cloud, of those whose work follows the legacies and genealogies of Leonard Peltier, have labored to put into geographical and political context the Oceti Oyate camp at Standing Rock in 2016 to 2017. Oceti Oyate became a site for another global Indigenous movement against settler disregard for treaty rights and history, against extractivist industries, and against the systemic racism and militarism that eventually allowed oil to flow inside the shell of the Dakota Access Pipeline.

As thousands of water protectors gathered at Oceti Oyate and other camps along Mni Sose (the Missouri River) at Cannon Ball, North Dakota, from April 2016 to February 2017, blankets, hides, and canvas provided shelter, security, and warmth. No guns, drugs, or alcohol were allowed at the camps, but the Morton County police, North Dakota state police, police units from neighboring counties and states, private security companies, and Tiger Swan agents used dogs, bullets, concussion grenades, helicopters, floodlights, and water as weapons to reinvigorate historical traumas and to enact new and ever-virulent forms. When security forces blasted water cannons at them, at night in below-freezing temperatures, water protectors shielded themselves with blankets.

UNFOLD 2

The blanket brings us into being—not only from the moment those of us born in hospitals were wrapped in the Kuddle Up blanket, manufactured by Medline, but throughout our lives as we acquire shells and take cover. In 1995, I visited portions of The NAMES Project AIDS Memorial Quilt, which were on display in my small hometown in South Dakota. HIV/AIDS was a distant problem (if a problem at all) to people in this town, but they knew quilts and quilting intimately—and thus the blanket uncovered an unspoken issue through a familiar form.

I volunteered at this event, but I remember nothing about my duties except that volunteers had to wear all white, which presented a problem for this rather morose teenager of the 1990s. I do remember that anyone who attended was invited to write a personal message on one of the blank quilt blocks. I knelt in those white jeans and chose a purple marker to write a message to my brother Kevin, or perhaps about Kevin. The gesture released something I hadn't anticipated—for years my grief had been escaping imperceptibly. Now, at seventeen, I had finally caught up to Kevin and then surpassed his age by one year. I was in uncharted territory. And I grieved for the queer self I knew I was to become: how disappointing and wasteful.

For years I wore a T-shirt I bought that evening; I wore it with all the queers in mind, my imagined community. But like the quilt, the T-shirt was a cover. It was white with a drawing of three children, two white and one African American, all standing and touching or holding blankets or corners of quilts. Without the phrase The NAMES Project AIDS Memorial Quilt emblazoned beneath, one would never connect the children and their blankets to HIV/AIDS, nor even to the NAMES Project. Partly visible text on one of the blankets appears to read "Keep the Love Alive." To whom is this declaration directed? Was it meant to remind those whose loves are dead not to forget them? I don't think they needed such a blanket message.

My grandmother crocheted blankets for each of us—several, actually. As we aged out of certain colors or sizes, another one would come along. I carried mine from room to room for three seasons of the year, one of the requests a house built in 1900 makes of its inhabitants. The blanket and I made our rounds, to visit older siblings who preferred us elsewhere, to curl up in a corner near a high-traffic area. I was an ethnographer of adulthood. But the blanket was most useful to lure my favorite companions—various cats I courted into domesticity from stray life, or our empathic Sheltie. My family even had a special rack for these blankets, though I remember that more often than not, the blankets were elsewhere—in use, or folded neatly across the top of a couch, or at the foot of a bed. Standing by.

Though I am obsessively tidy, there's nothing more inviting to me than a rumpled blanket on a couch. Certain blankets have a kind of muscle memory. Even without a human body underneath, they maintain the trace of habitation—a warm spot where a cat lay for hours, or a vertiginous crest where once there were bent knees. Kevin's blanket covered his wasting body, cancer-atrophied muscles and, I assume, the medical pads that my parents tried to hide from us.

What the blanket covered, it also made most conspicuous.

My dad and my oldest brother carried Kevin downstairs, from the bedroom he hadn't left for several weeks to the living room. It would be the last Christmas. They carried him in his recliner; his legs were covered with his blanket, his torso with a new button-down shirt and a slim black tie. For Christmas he received a Swatch. What did it mean to him to wear an instrument that measures time's passing?

He died thirty-two days after Christmas. In those intervening weeks, I don't remember Kevin speaking or eating, except the day of his best friend's last visit. Kevin greeted Shane, his words slurred but perceptible, and my mom made Kevin's favorite cupcakes, yellow cake with chocolate frosting. When it came time to choose his clothes for visitation and burial—Catholics repress the pleasures of life and train themselves to conceal, but feel no compunction about the display and hyper-visibility of death—Dad suggested we include Kevin's blanket in the coffin. We noticed then a glop of chocolate frosting embedded in the crochet stitch. Dad folded the blanket carefully in order not to disturb the frosting.

Kevin's body prone in a casket—blanket now folded neatly and deliberately to make the frosting visible—seemed to me, at least as I remember it now, to be twice removed from life: not just dead, but the utter negation of life. The goal, of course, is verisimilitude: just enough formaldehyde, makeup, hairspray, and concealed props to make the person look "like" themselves. The only part of the scene familiar to me was his blanket and its trace of a moment of pleasure for him.

I'm relieved they decided to bury that blanket. Who could have ever used it again? It would have become a relic in our home, like the bone fragments of a saint.

2 FOLDS

*One could know the beauty of the universe in each soul,
if one only could unfold all its folds, which only open
perceptibly with time.*

—G. W. LEIBNIZ, *PRINCIPLES OF GRACE*

From 1946 to 1970, the surface of Los Angeles transformed
as the tree population more than doubled—from 300,000 to
680,000—in step with the city's burgeoning population and
development.[1] Native species such as the California live oak
grow slowly and establish deep roots, but city developers
opted for fast-growing and dramatic giants whose buttress
root systems flare out from the base above ground: American
sweetgum, evergreen ash, southern magnolia, and Indian
laurel fig trees.[2] They lift and displace the concrete slab so
that the roots themselves form a sidewalk of entanglement.
Traversing certain sidewalks can feel like crossing a bridge
or navigating the slopes of a funnel where right angles no
longer rule.

The slow deterioration of a city's infrastructure, made especially visible in elevated, angled, and cracked sidewalks, or in potholes and obsolete bridges, draws attention to forms of urban cover: asphalt, grass, mulch, gravel, foundations, houses, pools, fountains (and all the concrete that keeps them disciplined), bridges, buildings, railroad tracks. Layers and layers of blankets. A sidewalk is a concrete blanket that covers layers of soil, sediment, rock, and roots. Tree roots threaten to disclose the sidewalk's secret: It is just a simple cover, and what's underneath will always rise to the fore, whether we want it to or not.

It was not woven wool or any textile that brought this chapter into being, but a slab of marble and folded concrete. The work of contemporary artist Analia Saban gave me permission to ask, *What is a blanket?* Saban consistently turns medium into material, material into medium, and space into time. With *The Painting Ball (48 Abstract, 42 Landscapes, 23 Still Lives, 11 Portraits, 2 Religious, 1 Nude)* (2005), Saban created a sphere comprised of unraveled paintings. She collected paintings from thrift stores, friends, fellow students, and Chinese painting factories, removed the stretchers, and unraveled the canvases. She then wound the combined threads into a 300-pound sphere. Saban confronts form by turning the flat weave of paintings into a sculptural object with density and mass.

By twisting and folding medium into matter, Saban transforms paint, concrete, marble, canvas, photographs, and domestic objects into encounters and conversations with art history, geology, time, lines, paint, cover, and blankets. *Fitted Bed Sheet* (2011) features a white, twin-sized fitted bed sheet with two corners tucked taut around the upper edge of a 78 ¼ × 44 × 5 ¼-inch canvas. The sheet hangs vertically, its upper plane smooth while mass and momentum gather creases and folds as the sheet descends the canvas. The sheet's lower corners, elastic and loose, fold into themselves to reveal the bottom edges of the canvas. The crescent trough reminds the viewer of how fitted sheets resist symmetry; a neatly folded fitted sheet requires folds within folds, and some elastic magic.

Fitted Bed Sheet confronts perspective and histories of representation by covering a canvas—a conventional medium for paint—with a sheet. But the cover does not wholly conceal the canvas, nor use the canvas as a mere prop for its own display. Rather, the materiality of the sheet brings the medium of the canvas into being because the sheet is made of acrylic paint—a trompe l'oeil pushed to the brink. Paint still covers canvas, but the encounter transforms acrylic into a fitted bed sheet and the canvas into a bed.[3] With the form of a recognizable domestic object, *Fitted Bed Sheet* turns comfort and familiarity strange. A bed sheet, familiar and mundane, conventionally made with organic materials and covered by a body, becomes a cover for pigment suspended in polymer.

Saban's art is not optical illusion, but camera obscura: projection and reversal, an interplay of darkness and light, internal and external, dimension and plane. In *Marking (from Porcelain Bathroom Sink)* (2014), a sink stands on the ground, tipped onto its left edge. The upper right corner of the sink is stripped away to reveal its hollow interior. On the wall to the right of the sink hangs a 96 × 70 ¼-inch linen canvas with a shock of ethereal white spray that travels upward from the corner nearest the sink. The exposure discloses a relation between the two media: Ground pigment from the porcelain sink makes the white paint for the canvas. The aligned edges of sink and canvas, and the continuous plane of white pigment, show how object and matter fold and unfold: the sink unfolds into the canvas, the canvas into art, and art into bathroom or bedroom. Far from inert and passive, the object—sheet, sink, canvas, paint—becomes duration, a complex happening in time and space. Folding and unfolding differentiate without inducing discontinuity. Matter, alive, inert, and even dead, folds into matter.

With Freudian resonance, Gilles Deleuze theorizes such material flexibility—the plasticity of the animate and inanimate—by regarding the folds of organisms, the interplay of endogenous and exogenous covers. "Folding-unfolding no longer simply means tension-release, contraction-dilation, but enveloping-developing, involution-evolution." When an organism dies, it *folds* into itself. "To unfold is to increase, to grow; whereas to fold is to diminish, to reduce, 'to withdraw into the recesses of a world'" (8–9). Folding and unfolding translate the movement or force of matter from one state to another. All organisms contain the possibility—the future unfolding—of other organisms.

Following Gottfried Wilhelm Leibniz, Deleuze thus breaks with Cartesian hierarchies. The "infinite exteriority of matter" folds "into the metaphysical principle of life and the physical law of phenomena" (Deleuze and Strauss, 233). The shell and its analogs (the cortical layer, bullet, convolute, blanket), whose exteriors are more visible and vulnerable to stimulation, protect and cover that which is interior and less visible or invisible. But exterior layers protect by mediation and cathexis, so that the relations between trauma and pleasure, death and life, inertia and animacy, exterior and interior, turn elastic.

Death comes to life along a crease—a topology, which Saban foregrounds in her *Draped Marble* series. Using commercially available marble slabs, Saban creates an emergent fold by breaking the marble slab down the center. She lines the endogenous fold with thin bent-steel plates that she fastens to wooden sawhorses, "faking the illusion of their malleability."[4] While I closely examined *Draped Marble (Fior di Pesco)* (2015) at the Marciano Museum in Los Angeles, a person looked at the fold from the other side and said, "Do you think it was an accident?" I immediately responded, "Oh no," not pausing to register whether she was serious. She laughed anyway. I was too overwhelmed by the exquisite engineering of this object to entertain a joke. But *Draped Marble* does look like an accident in the making—crumbled marble comprises the fold, which leaves the viewer to wonder if the longer it hangs there, the weaker it grows at the seam.

FIGURE 2 *Draped Marble (Fior di Pesco)* (2015) by Analia Saban.

Marble is a metamorphic rock composed of calcite or dolomite crystals, the result of sedimentary limestone heated and compressed. Limestone is formed by the decomposition and consolidation of calcareous marine organisms; fossil fragments are sometimes visible in limestone, which is more porous than marble. Sam Anderson frames his exploration of marble at the Calacata Borghini quarry in Carrara, Italy, in the heart of the Apuan Alps, as a long history of dramatic arcs and multiple scales: "The story of Italian marble is the story of difficult motion: violent, geological, haunted by failure and ruin and lost fortunes, marred by severed fingers, crushed dreams, crushed men." Marble's own composition, the "generations of tiny creatures [that] lived, died and drifted slowly to the bottom of a primordial sea," occupies a temporal scale that far exceeds humans. Marble is alive with death.

Like other materials that derive from fossilized creatures and plants, marble is a non-renewable resource. The crystalline stone can be polished to a soft sheen, and was the preferred material of Roman emperors, including Augustus, who "vowed to make it, instead of brick, the very fabric of Rome." As Norman Herz and David B. Wenner put it, "marble was the stone the master artisans could teach to speak" (14). And using isotopic signature techniques, geologists and archaeologists decipher the language and secrets embedded in marble's folds.[5] To excavate it from deep inside the earth, where it has lain for millions of years, is to touch nonhuman worlds and temporalities. To mine and transform marble into bathroom floors, kitchen counters, columns, cheese boards, and even furniture is to domesticate deep time. To search for specific marble varieties is to discover an expansive archive where consumers may peruse photos of massive marble slabs hanging in warehouses like carcasses in a locker. The website for ABC Stone in New York features a slideshow on its homepage of deep cuts from marble mountains in Italy— an ecological nightmare framed as consumer fantasy.

Saban's marble blankets call attention to the ubiquity of marble as a building material in contemporary homes and businesses—a signifier of opulence, yet readily available for home renovation. Marble paradoxically evokes both timelessness and disposability. In *Bathroom Sink Template (Jade Marble)* (2014), Saban mounts a 74 $^{11}/_{16}$ × 44-inch slab of marble vertically to a wall. On the lower end is an oval sink cutout, and the slab's top seam is jagged, like an edge of slate. The symmetrical oval parallel to the jagged edge demarcates two lives in one plane. Like the marble blankets, *Bathroom Sink Template* reorients the viewer's perspective, literally and ideologically: what is supposed to be flat and horizontal turns vertical and strange. The cutout for the sink appears impossibly small and distant, difficult to imagine. How is it that marble, made of fossils, heat, and grandeur, becomes the material for our bathrooms? As Saban herself put it to me, marble goes from "the majestic to the domestic."[6] The titles for each piece in the *Draped Marble* series provide a taxonomy of the marble and its provenance—*Fior di Pesco Carnico*, *Fior di Pesco Apuano*—reminding us that this extraordinary material came from elsewhere, places that most of us will never see in person.[7]

The marble of *Draped Marble* resembles a folded blanket. While it cannot provide warmth or even security (at least not for a human body), it folds and covers. With *Draped Concrete* (2016), a set of four consecutive concrete slabs draped over wooden sawhorses, Saban explores the blanket form with an entirely different material.

The concrete's folds form a similar tenuous rubble plane, but with cracks and faults that spider downward. The seams expose concrete interiors, inviting the viewer to notice the material's composition: an aggregate of broken stone with sand, cement, and water. *Draped Concrete* has dimension

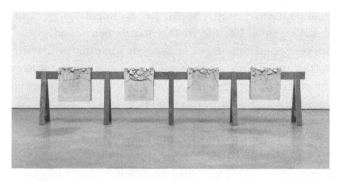

FIGURE 3 *Draped Concrete* (2016) by Analia Saban.

and scale that invite examination on a granular level and from multiple angles and sides. By breaking the horizontal plane and changing form and perspective, Saban's concrete blankets graft security to infrastructure, domestic spaces to sites of global extraction, and space to time. The blanket becomes a condensation and compression of time: the deep accumulation of years, dead organisms, uplift, and unfolding.[8]

Across his work on Leibniz and the Baroque, Deleuze tracks a theory of art unconfined to its own histories and conventions. That is, far from a delineated period of art history, Leibniz and Deleuze defer to the Baroque as a trope of "mystical experience . . . a fragility of infinitely varied patterns of movement," Tom Conley writes in his foreword to *The Fold* (x–xi). The Baroque best signifies the fold, the shape that itself signifies infinity. Folds order our material world, from the forms and structures we see and touch, like blankets, clothes, leaves, shells, and sedimentary layers, to invisible matter, like the air that folds when sound travels from one point to another. The Baroque is like the "protracted fascination we experience in watching waves heave, tumble, and atomize when they crack along an unfolding line being traced along the expanse of a shoreline" (x).

A companion series to *Draped Concrete*, Saban's *Folded Concrete* (2017) features thick, folded concrete blankets that rest on walnut pallets. Each of the three blankets in the installation is folded and titled according to common paper folds: "Three-Fold," "Zig-Zag Fold," and "Gate Fold." Not until I encountered *Draped Concrete* and *Folded Concrete* did sidewalks, asphalt streets, and even cities become blankets. The blanket's cracks, faults, and rubble seam are at once familiar because I encounter the deterioration of concrete (and related materials, such as asphalt) in my everyday life when sidewalks crack and lift, or potholes and impressions emerge; yet the concrete is no longer under my feet as sidewalk or flooring, but in my line of vision and in the form of a blanket.

Saban's art takes the form beyond itself to animate the fold and unfold. By creating a kind of emergency in the material—the appearance of cracked and crumbling marble or concrete signifies imperial or urban deterioration and destruction—Saban induces an ontological transformation. Marble and concrete are blankets of a becoming, blankets already with long histories comprised of multiple lives and deaths, under pressure and compression, made possible by amalgamation. Like their raw, unblanketed forms, *Draped*

FIGURE 4 *Folded Concrete (Gate Fold)* 2017 by Analia Saban.

Marble and *Draped Concrete* are timekeepers; their folds and creases store millennia, generations, and catastrophes. They are sedimentary covers. When Saban turns a slab of marble into a fractured and folded blanket, the draped marble *is* and *represents*—in a Deleuzian sense, it is both being and becoming. The blanket form is an unfold: the matter and medium that presents another time and place. This marble could be mined from the Apuan Alps in Italy, a riverbed in Brazil, or from one of the twenty-one quarries in Afghanistan; and it's also *from*, as in formed by, limestone buried deep in the earth's crust which has been subjected to heat and pressure.[9] The blanket derives from multiple bodies and times; it comes into being under multiple hands. To encounter the marble blanket's matter and soul—not only its veins, faults, and contours, but its "blanketness"—is to transmute time, space, labor, and metaphor.

The phrase *living under a rock* suggests someone is naive, out of touch, perhaps a little backward, whereas to *hide under a blanket*, as practice or metaphor, is to protect oneself, to guard against the realities of life. Rocks and blankets, two forms of cover, are meant to register entirely distinct forms of affective engagement with the world. But through the fold—both form and concept—Saban's concrete and marble blankets graft geology to textile, and the vast scale of time, life, and death to a form of cover and protection.

Freud could have used *convolute* as a substitute for cortical layer; in geological terms, convolute means coiled or wound together, "as in a gastropod shell whose inner whorls are entirely concealed by the outer whorls" (Bates and Jackson, 111). *Convolute bedding* (also convolute lamination) refers to intricately woven or folded sediment (silt or fine sand) or sedimentary rock that is confined to a layer, "dies out both upward and downward," and then is covered by parallel undisturbed layers. Convolute bedding resembles a layered topography of lines and tracks, wrinkled folds like an unmade bed, an interplay of geology and geometry. A crumpled piece of paper resembles mountain peaks and river valleys because these geological and topographical features go through the same process—of buckling, compressing, folding, and unfolding.

To stand on a vista overlooking a city is to glimpse urban geometry. A certain point of view brings forth all possible connections between one point of the city and another. "The city seems to be a labyrinth that can be ordered. The world is an infinite series of curvatures or inflections" (Deleuze 24). To stand at another point, particularly above or below the original point, is to shift perspective and scale and thus apprehend an entirely different city of folds. But each view offers the entirety of the city: an infinite series of folds within folds. Leibniz pushes the city metaphor to its limit to suggest that in the metamorphic, spongy, and cavernous creases and folds of a city, we see an infinite folding and unfolding that orders the soul: the "entire world is enclosed in the soul from one point of view" (Deleuze 24).

Leibniz also reckons with the correspondence between the "coils of matter" and the "folds in the soul," by invoking the metaphor and matter of veins in marble:

> Sometimes the veins are the twisted coils of matter which surround the living beings caught in the block, so that a bank of marble is like an undulating lake full of fish. Sometimes the veins are the innate ideas in the soul, like the bent figures or the potential statues caught in a block of marble. Matter is marbled, and the soul is marbled, in two different ways. (Deleuze and Strauss, 229)

The veins of marble are both analogy and matter: Marble is a mass of compressed folds, deep time and once-living beings now caught in a block, and its soul vibrates with the potential to become something else.[10] The marble *stores* a becoming statue. Or blanket.

Throughout *The Fold*, Deleuze makes use of analogy and metaphor—sometimes his own (the fan, or a reading of Mallarmé), but also as invocation of Leibniz's own metaphors (the city, veins of marble). Given the very notion of the fold—the autonomy of interiority and the infinite exteriority of matter—the metaphors turn material at any given point. For instance, to explain Leibniz's theory of elasticity, a body's degree of hardness and fluidity, Deleuze likens the compressive forces that work on matter to a boat's high speed that causes a wave to become as hard as a marble wall. With metaphor, the principle of elasticity comes to life: waves like marble. And at the same time, the waves, the boat, marble, and speed are all materially structured by folds.[11] Marble appears again in perhaps the most well-known figure of Leibniz's Baroque: the house (sometimes a chamber or chapel) with two floors. Its upper floor, analogous to the soul, contains a room in black marble. Light "enters only through orifices so well bent that nothing on the outside can be seen through them, yet they illuminate or color the décor of a pure inside" (Deleuze 28). Though it appears opaque, the marble filters light through its imperceptible openings, its animate folds and compressions.

Layli Long Soldier's (Lakota) poem "Vaporative" contends with the folding of light into matter with a similar interplay between opacity and animate or organic bodies. The poem begins:

> However a light may come
> through vaporative
> glass pane or dry dermis
> of hand winter bent
> I follow that light
> capacity that I have (23)

Light filters through transparent and opaque surfaces, glass to skin—a capacity and momentum carried and grounded by the subjective body. Later, the form shifts to prose to confront an incongruous relation between light and language. "I have wanted *opaque* to mean see-through, transparent. I'm disheartened to learn it means the opposite. . . . To say, I'm interested in this painting on glass brightly opaque" (27). The speaker contends with language as an ordering, "a need for stability," against the propulsions of her own luminous instinct. Where she wants *opaque* to mean *transparent* resides the fold: "I negotiate instinct when a word of lightful meaning flips under / buries me in the work of blankets" (27). The slash between "under" and "buries"—the signal of a line break without imposing the break itself—formalizes the fold. Light folds into blanket, a surface goes under cover.

Long Soldier anticipates the fold of "dry dermis" or glass pane—each filters light, though one is opaque and the other transparent. As with Leibniz's marble, either way, light has a capacity to move through. In another description of the Baroque chamber, the room of the soul contains only a stretched canvas, *as if it were a living dermis*—the intimate crease between organic and inorganic matter (4). And paintings on the canvas make use of shadow so that "things jump out of the background [and] figures are defined by their covering more than their contours" (31–32). Leibniz must have seen a ghost in that house.

UNFOLD 3

Our house was not merely a building that contained our family, but was itself another kind of soul. It was crowded with ghosts who made themselves present to me nearly every night. And later, it nearly suffocated us with our own sorrow. But in the years before Kevin died in his room, despite the nightly terrors that sent my blanket and me on the search for corporeal companionship, I preferred that house over friends. Or rather, I didn't bother to make friends because I had that house. When new adults crossed its threshold, I asked if they would like a tour. Rather than an expressed devotion to its Victorian architecture, or a childish desire to briefly court an alien adult into my world, my invitation was the fulfillment of a social obligation, like introducing two friends at a cocktail party. On my regular circuit, I pointed out the house's original woodwork and door knobs mated with skeleton keys.

While Kevin was in treatment or undergoing surgery in Denver, my parents lived at the Ronald McDonald House. It was a 1911 Victorian on Colfax Avenue, not far from the Cathedral Basilica of the Immaculate Conception, where they surely went to church every Sunday. Perhaps they also stopped in from time to time to plead for a different narrative, a radical shift in the trajectory of their son's cancer.

They let me stay with them in Denver for a few days. My first introduction to the Ronald McDonald House was at night—I think we entered through the galley kitchen. In my memory, the light was blue, as if the kitchen were illuminated only by an aquarium. We passed a person who carried a dish, or was it a pizza box or takeout, into the kitchen. Her skin was blue. The ghosts back at home were more alive and present than she was. She had entered the dimension of illness where time stretches to a seemingly endless expanse until it snaps back and contracts with violence and force: a constant negotiation between *when will this end* and *too soon.* Maybe we said hello, but I know I felt a jolt at the experience of entering a house (which looked like the distant city cousin of mine) that was occupied by people other than my own family. The house was only pretending to be home, and it was rife with little signifiers of its betrayal: a handwritten but official sign reminding people to wash their dishes; competing smells in the kitchen; commercial carpeting and industrial rubber thresholds; the collective grief of strangers. There were blankets folded on the backs of couches and chairs, stacked in the corners, tucked into closets.

3 EXTRACTION

When Ted Kuntz presented a blanket to *Antiques Roadshow* appraiser Donald Ellis, a "tribal arts" expert, he had no idea that the object he inherited from his grandmother would be one of the most valuable items ever to appear on the popular PBS show. Following the general format and script, Ellis asks Kuntz a few perfunctory questions to heighten the moment's drama: "And do you know who made this weaving, do you know what kind of blanket it is?" and "So you haven't had anybody look at it or . . .?"[1] Ellis admits to Kuntz that the blanket caught his breath at first sight. He concludes that the object before them is a Navajo (Diné)-made First Phase Chief blanket. "These were made in about 1840 to 1860 and it's called a Ute, First Phase." "A Ute?" Kuntz asks. "A Ute First Phase wearing blanket," responds Ellis. And Kuntz repeats, "A Ute First Phase wearing blanket."

Chief blankets, Diné weaver Joyce Begay-Foss explains, are the most recognized nineteenth-century Diné textiles. Woven with banded stripes of off-white and brown with wool from churro sheep, "early chief blankets were usually worn by prominent individuals or persons of stature, especially among the Ute, Comanche, and Plains Indians, with whom the Diné frequently traded" (Tisdale 25). The Diné acquired indigo from Mexico, which allowed them to experiment with blue. First Phase Ute-style chief blankets like the one on *Antiques Roadshow* balance blue and brown stripes at both ends.

Kuntz confesses that he doesn't know "an awful lot about" the blanket. He grew up with it on the foot of the bed in his grandmother's home, and in his home, he stored it on the back of a chair. But according to family history, the blanket once belonged to Kit Carson. And, he adds, "I'm sure everybody knows his history."

The Treaty of Guadalupe Hidalgo in 1848—which officially ended the Mexican-American War and by which Mexico ceded to the United States present-day Arizona and New Mexico, parts of Utah, Nevada, and Colorado, and all claims to Texas—also conditioned a settler sense of Diné as especially "savage" because of their "raids." Of course, those who settled in this newly colonized territory did not recognize the land as Diné Bikéyah, Navajo homelands, and that *they*, the settlers, were the invaders and intruders. For a dozen years, the US government seemed to give little thought to the original inhabitants of its newly acquired territory, but in 1860, the Army justified the use of force against Diné in response to increasing tensions. In 1862, General James Carlton proposed a removal and relocation plan to forcibly move Navajo and Apache people to Bosque Redondo, or what the Diné call Hwéeldi, in New Mexico, near Fort Sumner (Bsumek 24). He selected Christopher "Kit" Carson to carry out the plan and gave Carson full license to kill anyone who resisted. As Traci

Brynne Voyles explains, the "larger U.S. campaign had one goal: to rout the Navajos from their homeland and march them some 300 miles southeast" to Bosque Redondo. This was, "for all intents and purposes, a military concentration camp" (vii). By 1865, 8,000 Diné had endured the Long Walk to Fort Sumner; one quarter of the population died along the way.

Navajo leaders negotiated their first treaty with the US government in 1868, which established initial boundaries for the reservation—only about one quarter of Diné Bikéyah. The treaty offered "provisions": white teachers, farming supplies, sheep, goats, and cattle. In turn, the Navajo Nation conceded to the construction of railroads and military posts on their reservation lands. All the while, Diné women never stopped weaving—the forced march, imprisonment, and railroads manifest in their designs.

Spider Woman (Na ashje'ii'Asdzáá) lives at Spider Rock, an 800-foot sandstone formation at the heart of the Navajo Nation, which the Diné call Tséyi' and settlers call Canyon de Chelly. Spider Woman taught Diné women how to weave, and according to Diné origin stories, weaving is a matter of survival. Weaving reflects *hózhóó* from Diné cosmology and lifeways—the concepts and restoration of balance, beauty, harmony, and order. Designs reflect the individual weaver's sensibility, her way of seeing the world, and a kind of world-making that manifests *hózhóó* for humans and nonhumans.[2] Contemporary weaver D. Y. Begay explains that part of living and practicing a traditional Navajo lifestyle is to recognize that plants, animals, the earth and the sky have voices that are "transmitted through the atmosphere. The deities of these natural elements wait for the earth people to speak to them and to request permission to collect the plants and to extract pigments to create colors for our weavings."[3] Begay's rug *Dah iisló Bizaad* (Weaving's Voice) incorporates natural dyes to evoke the mesas and sandstone of the Southwest.

Contemporary artist Will Wilson (Diné), who learned weaving from his grandmother, calls his 2011 beaded rug *eyeDazzler* a "trans-customary collaborative expression."

FIGURE 5 *eyeDazzler: Trans-customary Portal to Another Dimension* (2011) by Will Wilson.

This project, a collaboration with Diné weavers Joy Farley and Pamela Brown, took over 1,000 hours of labor and 76,050 glass beads to complete. It follows Diné designs and weaving practices, except at the center of the blanket where two beaded QR codes appear. The full title of the piece, *eyeDazzler: Trans-customary Portal to Another Dimension*, fulfills its promise: scanning the QR code links to an online short film Wilson co-created with Dylan McLaughlin (Diné).[4]

The film opens with a split screen and close-ups of a woven wool Navajo blanket whose pattern resembles precisely Wilson's beaded creation, without the QR code. We hear Wilson's mother, Lola Etsitty, and his aunt, Margaret Edgewater, discussing the original "two-faced"/two-sided rug "Eyedazzler." Then one panel of the screen shifts to a computer screen where we see the pattern rendered in pixels; the other side offers a close-up of the beaded version. The diegetic conversation continues through several scene shifts that feature the project's collaborators—a moving headshot— next to shots of their hands weaving or sorting beads. They stand still and gaze at the viewer through the camera, as if they've been asked to pose for a photograph, but most break and smile or laugh—some dart their eyes. The final shot in this sequence is of Wilson, whose gaze also breaks. He looks down and rubs his hand.

eyeDazzler embodies a temporal assemblage, where inherited practices and designs merge with new media. In this sense, the blanket carries on the traditions of Diné weaving, a practice where experimentation is, in fact, innate to the tradition, and thus the tradition always innovates. The title cites the Eyedazzler style of the late nineteenth century, when weavers experimented with synthetic dyes on hand-spun or Germantown yarn. Wilson patterned his co-creation on an Eyedazzler rug made by Martha Etsitty, his grandmother, around 1976. The echo of Etsitty's work resounds even in Wilson's title, though as with any echo or repeated form, the copy is not exact—and Wilson cites this as well, where the lower-case *e* and upper-case *D* refer to the blanket's new media.[5]

Wilson decided to compose his rug with beads, rather than wool, after seeing Erica Lord's *Diabetes Burden Strap, DNA Microarray Analysis* (2008).[6] Lord (Athabaskan and Iñupiaq) codes the genetic marker for diabetes with Japanese glass beads on a burden strap, an Athabaskan object that supports a baby from underneath so that a mother can carry the baby on her back. Lord explains that burden straps are "generally heavily beaded and adorned."[7] A microarray DNA analysis tests one's genetic predisposition for certain diseases, including diabetes, which disproportionately affects Native people.[8] By coding a genetic marker for disease on a traditional Athabaskan object used to carry babies, Lord grafts two different forms of inheritance and reproduction: one a matter of kinship and biological reproduction, the other a reproduction of disease that accompanies poverty and lack of access to health care and nourishing food, direct results of ongoing colonialism.[9] Both *eyeDazzler* and *Diabetes Burden*

Strap, DNA Microarray Analysis are indebted to inheritance, and each is a kind of *carrier*. Lord's burden strap makes this especially clear with the notion of *predisposition*, where one's own body turns carrier.

Ted Kuntz was "flabbergasted" and teary to learn from *Antiques Roadshow* that his blanket could be appraised between $350,000 and $500,000. After he recovered from the news, he explained to Ellis that his family was made up of "poor farmers." His grandmother's foster father "had started some gold mills and discovered gold and everything, but there was no wealth. No wealth in the family at all." The blanket Kuntz presents carries the accumulation of histories: the chief or revered person to whom the blanket originally belonged, Kit Carson, The Long Walk, churro sheep, and in the Kuntz family, a connection between his grandmother and Kit Carson—a "frontiersman by the name of Mark Bedell," almost certainly the same person who operated a trading post for buffalo hides near Fort Lyon, Colorado, where Carson died in 1868.[10] Bedell's operation (where hunters could spend the night by spreading "their blankets on piles of hides"), Carson, the extraction of gold, and farming uncover histories and tactics by which settlers accumulate their wealth through eliminatory strategies (genocide and removal, extermination of bison) and land dispossession.[11] Kuntz's family may never have been wealthy by certain standards, and Kuntz himself did not assume a luxurious lifestyle after selling the blanket—he used the money to pay off his mortgage and to cover health expenses. Nevertheless, the specific conditions and circumstances under which Kit Carson gave Bedell the blanket, which Kuntz eventually inherited from his grandmother whose foster father extracted gold, represent colonial histories folded in on themselves. *Antiques Roadshow* never needs to unfold the details of these histories, or the histories of Navajo weaving, Ute people and trading practices, or Kit Carson (after whom a town near Fort Lyon is named), because the blanket is worth hundreds of thousands of dollars, and that is the only inheritance that matters in this exchange.[12]

In a subsequent interview, Kuntz described the desire to collect "old things"—"we just want to know where we came from, I guess." But when settlers collect blankets, baskets, crib boards, burden straps, pottery, headdresses, and pipes (to name a few examples), and pass them on to their descendants, they willfully or inadvertently *refuse* their own histories. To *pass down* and *inherit* is to accumulate wealth, and wealth can afford to conceal histories and ongoing colonial-induced crises, such as Bosque Redondo, starvation and death, uranium mining, the atomic bomb, and contaminated water. But artists like Will Wilson and Erica Lord use the blanket and textile to unfold these histories: weaving and beading practices handed down through generations, and the conditions of inheritance and circumstance by which a body becomes predisposed to disease. Blankets witness and carry these histories, and Wilson and Lord provide the codes to decipher them, while settlers depend on the blanket's silence and secrets.

At the center of Jeanine Oleson's *Conduct Matters* installation at the Hammer Museum in Los Angeles (2017) lies a hand-woven rug. *Perspectus . . . a . . . um* (2017) is a light-gray square with a plaid-like grid of woven black bars that contract at one end and widen at the other. Amid this grid, one green bar and one red bar meet in the shape of a large L. Installed in the center of a small, dimly lit gallery, the rug or blanket appears to be innocuous.

On one wall of the room plays the three-channel film *Crossed Wires* (2017). Up against an adjacent wall, a small monitor runs another film, *Ground* (2017). A thick copper wire protrudes from the center of this monitor. Like a needle under the skin to draw blood, the copper is inserted into thick hand-cast glass, an overlay on the monitor's surface. On the floor to the left of the monitor sits a large terra-cotta, wood, and brass gramophone, *Matter-phone* (2016). The copper tubing from the monitor weaves behind the gramophone and meets up with other lines of tubing connected to it.

Ground offers a montage of scenes and images, bound by the presence of copper. Footage plays from Bloomberg News, complete with the crawl of stock losses. An anchor's face flashes up briefly, then cuts to a moving image of a rocky terrain with the caption "BHP Union disagree over pay offer." The copper wire disrupts the view. The scene shifts again to a computer-generated 3D image of a topography that resembles a deep canyon, which reveals itself as an aerial view of a massive open-pit mine. *Ground* then returns to Bloomberg News footage. Periodically, the same 3D topography appears

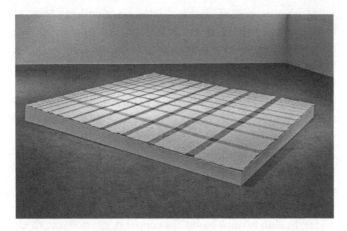

FIGURE 6 *Perspectus . . . a . . . um* (2017) by Jeanine Oleson.

FIGURE 7 *Conduct Matters* (2017) by Jeanine Oleson.

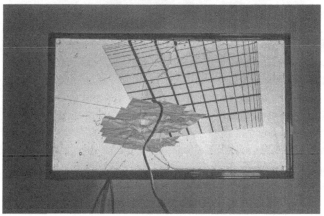

FIGURES 8 and 9 *Ground* (2017) by Jeanine Oleson.

and shifts position—the viewer notices a computer cursor moving, suggesting the agency and presence of another. A 3D model of the installation's woven blanket appears on the screen, and the cursor moves it a few times until it overlaps with the rocky topography. In one scene, the topography juts through the blanket and covers the mine. As we watch a user work the textile in this imaging platform, we see through its "fibers" and grid into a copper mine.

The blanket's title *Perspectus . . . a . . . um* refers to the declension of the Latin transitive verb *perspicio* (*perspectus, perspecta, perspectum*)—to see through, to examine, to observe—and these are the very actions into which *Ground* courts its viewers. The blanket both covers the mine, but also allows us to see through it at points—not quite transparent, it covers just enough to draw our attention to the ground underneath. And as we watch the film, we stand proximate to the protrusion of copper tubing that could have been mined from that very site: Its dimension and scale emerge, literally, from the screen. At a certain point in *Ground*, as we see the blanket grid vertically oriented and moving down into the topography, the scene shifts abruptly to four of Oleson's collaborators (and actors in *Crossed Wires*) busily working around a table together to make the gramophone, and to hammer the copper wires we now have next to us and around us in the present moment of viewing.

Sounds, which almost resemble someone bumping the wall on the other side of the gallery, reverberate at certain intervals from *Matter-phone*. Oleson transferred the labors figured in *Ground*, including hands hammering copper and the clicking of a computer mouse, to *Matter-phone* via a low frequency tactical transducer speaker.[13] The sound produced is low and physical. From these images of hands working and cursors moving, accompanied by sounds out of sync with their actions, the viewer gets a sense of labor's transmission and alienation. Much of the film in general is concerned with labor and materiality. For instance, the blanket's grid is based on the "platter" or ground that orients virtual objects in 3D imaging platforms, such as the one that appears in motion in *Ground*.[14] Like Wilson's *eyeDazzler, Perspectus . . . a . . . um* is digitally designed, but also handmade: The blanket comes into being by a co-production of media forms and weaving practices. And the flash of captions and clips— "BHP Union disagree over pay offer," "BHP Billiton stock down .68 points"—refer to the February 2017 strike at the Escondida copper mine in Chile, owned and operated by Anglo-Australian conglomerate BHP Billiton, when workers began a 43-day strike over the onerous terms of their new three-year contract.

Oleson maintains "a physical process of making as a mode of thinking, and that's what the speaker, wire, glass, and weaving provided."[15] *Conduct Matters* exposes viewers to the labor of making art, and the enmeshed relations at work in their act of watching or consuming it: the copper in the television monitor (and in our phones and computers) and the wire jutting out from the screen depend on a miner's labor, on the constant extraction of precious minerals from the earth. The workers' strike and the artists at work make visible what is otherwise alienated and hidden from view. Meanwhile, the blanket covers, but never fully conceals, the open-pit mine. Its own patterns are fashioned from the grid that orients virtual 3D objects. The platform and grid make possible our view of the virtual mine.

As you stand to watch *Ground*, with *Perspectus . . . a . . . um* lying resolute and currently inert behind, you may be drawn to or distracted by the narration and images from *Crossed Wires* in separate (though sometimes continuous) channels across the perpendicular wall. In one sequence, a character played by Lisa Reynolds, a member of Oleson's four-person ensemble, takes a tour of the Mission Mine, an open-pit mine south of Tucson, AZ. A tour guide explains to the group (who appear to all be white and middle-aged to elderly, except for Reynolds) how the extraction process works. Her matter-of-fact tone, tinged with excitement and didacticism, almost makes the process seem obvious or natural—until the images of the ravaged mine itself reappear. Reynolds then boards a bus—we hear the tour narration continue—and the group pulls up to an overlook above the open pit. Reynolds treats the scene as if it were land art, an earthwork. She asks the tour guide, "So how are you making decisions on the shape . . . the . . . terraces?" The tour guide gives her a puzzled look, but gamely responds with an elementary and gestural explanation of how the layers are blasted away, one fold at a time: "They start up at the top, blasted all that one layer, then blast the next layer."

Earlier in the film, Reynolds stands behind a chain-link fence with the mine in distant view. She delivers a lecture about land art, labor, and geological time to three other characters who listen carefully, but fail to follow her logic. Reynolds calls the mine a "monumental earthwork, or land art, as I like to call it." If we were to account for the history of land art, she explains, we see how this work—the mine— "refers directly back to the topography of the geological time before an era of extraction. This way of looking at time lends itself to a calm and reflective approach. Can you feel it?" The irony, of course, is that extraction has made possible the stark visibility of geological time—layers blasted away to reveal folds "of winds, of waters, of fire and earth, and subterranean folds of veins of ore in a mine" (Deleuze 6).

Oleson brings the blanket and rocks, minerals, and elements into a mode of intimate exchange. The blanket and copper are conductive materials: Blankets conduct thermal energy, and copper conducts electricity. Blankets also have an electric energy—the sparks visible in the dark, or hair that stands on end, a little work of electron magic. When *Perspectus . . . a . . . um* interacts with the mine, it reminds us that elements like copper and gold, or resources like oil and water, cover or layer in the land like blankets. And like a blanket, they store energy: the potential to warm and cool our homes, fuel our cars, and make bombs to destroy the world.

Ted Kuntz's family may have "discovered" gold in Colorado, but another yellow rock would later be mined and extracted from Diné Bikéyah. Leslie Marmon Silko's 1977 novel

Ceremony contends with the background of atomic lifecycles on stolen lands, the manufacturing of bombs from the rocks folded into mesas. The narrative follows Tayo, a Laguna Pueblo World War II veteran, whose return from war leaves him in the throes of trauma. While in a Philippines jungle, Tayo witnesses the death of his brother Rocky, and this, along with the scale of combat violence, leaves him wracked with guilt. He thinks he should have been killed instead of Rocky, and he's consumed with the notion that in turn, he might have killed Japanese soldiers—the delusions and disorientation caused by his trauma leave him unsure. Tayo returns to Laguna with a sense that he is responsible for his family's suffering and for the severe drought their lands now endure.

With the help of Betonie, a Diné and Mexican healer and keeper of stories and ceremony, Tayo confronts his trauma; in the final stages of his healing ceremony, Tayo walks to a mineshaft, where he finds ore,

> gray stone streaked with powdery yellow uranium, bright and alive as pollen; veins of sooty black formed lines with the yellow, making mountain ranges and rivers across the stone. But they had taken these beautiful rocks from deep within the earth and they had laid them in a monstrous design, realizing destruction on a scale only *they* could have dreamed. (229)

The passage indirectly calls into contrast the patterns of weavings and blankets that manifest *hózhóó*—which incorporate the landscape, rocks, and plants materially and spiritually into a design—with a settler-colonial pattern that dreams up destruction by extraction.

Blankets witness and play a hand in Tayo's trauma and his healing: Rocky is carried, injured and dying, through the jungle in a blanket, a makeshift stretcher. When Tayo returns home and lies sick in bed, he watches Auntie change the sheets and blankets from all the beds, as if "Rocky still slept there, tucking the dark wool blankets around the corners of the clean sheets, stuffing the pillows into starched white pillowcases she had ironed the day before" (28). Much later, when he registers that the effects of trauma have loosened, the narrator compares the change to an "unraveling like the yarn of a dark heavy blanket wrapped around a corpse" (184). A blanket worn by Ts'eh, Tayo's lover and healer— who is perhaps not fully human, or alive in the corporeal sense—bears a woven design that enacts the patterns of land: white and gray storm clouds, black lightning, brown wind (165). Ts'eh also works intently with rocks, including "ocher yellow sandstone with a powdery fine texture he had never seen before" (170). Ts'eh's touch and patterns, her blanket, stones, and bundles of freshly gathered plants and tobacco, become part of Tayo's healing from the traumas of war, from Trinity Site at White Sands, from laboratories on lands stolen from Cochiti Pueblo in the Jemez Mountains where the top-secret plans were made. At Laguna, he is at least 300 miles away from Trinity Site, and only proximate to Diné Bikéyah where more uranium is extracted. But in the mineshaft, Tayo begins to see the connections, the dismantled boundaries, and the distances across space and time unified by the rocks the "destroyers" (white settlers) work into patterns that turn people into shadows in "cities twelve thousand miles away, victims who had never known these mesas, who had never seen the delicate colors of the rocks which boiled up their slaughter" (228).

In the years following the bombing of Hiroshima and Nagasaki, the US Federal Civil Defense Administration, in collaboration with the public schools of Astoria, NY, created the short film *Duck and Cover* to teach children how to protect themselves in case of an atomic bomb strike. The film begins with a "very alert" animated turtle named Bert who knows just what to do when danger strikes: He folds into his shell, to *duck and cover*. "We all know the atomic bomb is very dangerous," the narrator explains, and so we all must learn to duck and cover to protect ourselves, like Bert. The nine-minute film features a long montage of white children engaged in "normal" activities—playing outside, riding a bike, or walking down the hall in school—but when an intense flash strikes, the children collapse to the ground and cover their heads with their hands, books, and newspapers. In one sequence, a family enjoys a picnic, complete with a blanket spread out to hold an assortment of plates. And then the flash. The quick-thinking Son grabs the corners of the blanket, and in one Houdini motion, the blanket turns into a shell, a protective layer against the atomic bomb.[16]

UNFOLD 4

I recently spent three hours feverishly scrolling through my digital photo archives to validate a memory I have of an image—not even a memory of a moment I experienced directly, but one distilled and deferred. It would have been taken on May 12, 2010, after my grandma passed away in her bed at home. Her body lay underneath multiple blankets, and on top of those rested her orange cat, still holding vigil and keeping watch. I remember receiving that photo from my mom, but I remember nothing else after that. Did I save it? After these hours of searching, I could only find a gap: photos taken of my daily life (the dogs snuggled up on the couch, morning coffee) before she died, and then nothing until several days after the funeral, when my parents and I visited Kevin's grave and our old house, the site of my childhood hauntings.

I have only one handwritten letter from Kevin. He wrote me from the hospital in Denver on our mom's stationery. "That's why it's all flowery," he explained in the first line. He asked how our Sheltie Josh was doing, and if I'd been playing pool with Grandma and Grandpa. Indeed, we played several times a week in the evenings while we watched our programs. Their house turned into my primary residence, and they my primary caretakers for a period of Kevin's illness. In certain intervals from ages five to eight, I became accustomed to their rhythms, their morning and bedtime rituals, and the epic family tragedies that unfolded on *Dallas* every Friday night.

I did find this photo from a bitter cold Christmas Eve in South Dakota. I'm thirty-two, sitting between my grandparents and parents on a couch that my parents handed down to Brian, my oldest brother—a plush time machine shuttled from childhood. My dad has their dog on his lap, and I have my dog Sylvan on mine. I remember how Sylvan decided to jump up and settle in. I remember feeling at home and relaxed, safe and secure. And I remember a look on my grandma's face that I had never quite seen—melancholy, wistful, quiet, but still a joyful spark. The act of taking her photograph was the only thing that could momentarily still her. She was always animated and talking. She even whispered to her pans, measuring cups, and food while she cooked. But here, in this photograph, she was placid. She hooked her arm in my grandpa's, and then reached over to put her hand on my dog, a way of reaching out to me too. I remember thinking, *This is her last Christmas*. I knew even then that this was a moment to take in and keep close, that we would never again assemble quite like this—that thought a flash now archived. The photo is blurry because I had the camera on the wrong setting, and I was aware of this when I handed it to Brian. But I didn't want to waste anyone's time by readjusting. We're all a little ghostly.

While Kevin was still in treatment, I remember that his doctor told my parents she was leaving town for Hawai'i, a much-needed vacation. But that was just a cover. Instead, she killed herself. I met her once on a trip to Denver, and she took me aside by myself, into a bright fluorescent room. She explained the concept of a cell, the difference between red blood cells and white cells, and then used slides to show me how cancer cells reproduce and cover the body. Sometimes they enter bones, like the femur and spine. Kevin and my parents initially thought he had injured his leg playing football. He was twelve. He dressed up as an injured football player for Halloween because he was on crutches anyway. It turned out, the cancer—Ewing's Sarcoma—was just waiting there.

Just a few months ago, I mentioned the doctor's death to my parents and they looked confused because Kevin's doctor never died. It was the hospital's social worker assigned to us. I could have easily changed *doctor* to *social worker* here—the rest is the same—but why did I misremember that detail? For Walter Benjamin, memory is a matter of archaeology, a medium rather than an instrument for exploring the past. Excavations must be planned carefully, but no "less indispensable is the cautious probing of the spade in the dark loam" (576). The memory is one thing, but the precise location from which one extracts it, the loam and strata through which one mines the past, is perhaps the "richest prize."

What was it, really, that I hoped to encounter in the digging for that photo? If I had found it, would it only have confirmed this memory of a photo, or would it have reminded me how distorted and distressed memories actually are? I think of the photo as an inventory of blankets. But maybe, if I were to see it again, it would take me back to grief, the site of its possession. Oh but no, the grief is still here, epic and rhapsodic.

4 SECURITY

For sure, they don't want you ever to get comfortable.
Nor do they ever want you to have a sense of security.
And, for sure, you don't. Security's the one thing you
never get in a maximum-security prison.
—LEONARD PELTIER, PRISON WRITINGS

In 1993, the World Health Organization directed the UN
Refugee Agency (UNHRC) to stop transporting food to
war-torn Sarajevo for two weeks, and to deliver clothing and
blankets instead. Though the winter had been relatively mild,
temperatures could drop to −20° C (−4° F) at night—inside a
building. On his travels to evaluate public health conditions
in Bosnia, Sir Donald Acheson, former chief medical officer
for England, encountered a surgeon at the state hospital in
Sarajevo who woke up each morning "with his face frozen"
despite covering himself with all available blankets. There
was no coal, fuel oil, or electricity in the city. A team from
the WHO, with aid from the Finnish Army, determined that

at −10° C, a person would need 8 CLO, which is the thermal insulation rating of "indoor clothing plus outdoor clothing plus average sleeping bag plus two blankets." Covered with "a good blanket" for ten hours per day, a person with only indoor clothing saves the energy equivalent to 3 kilograms of body fat per month.[1] The committee determined refugees needed blankets more than food.

In the wake and receding of Hurricane Harvey in Texas and Louisiana, residents and rescuers discovered death: not only corpses and the remains of those who did not escape, but also the figurative skeletons of their own previous lives. Among the visual archives from this disaster are photographs from evacuation centers. From the overhead shots, one gets a sense of the destruction's vast scale—the endless rows of green cots, some empty, others occupied by amorphous shapes. White blankets with "American Red Cross" and its logo cover cots and bodies: a test pattern of disaster, distress, and exhaustion. The Lake Charles Civic Center in Lake Charles, Louisiana, sheltered evacuees, and in one photo from this site, an assemblage of blankets covers mostly unoccupied cots. The blankets and sheets communicate allegiance to sports—one blanket is covered in the recognizable symbols of baseball, soccer, and football, and another pillowcase features a large image of a tiger's head in gold and purple for the LSU Tigers. Other blankets are piled and rumpled, cast aside or neatly stacked. In the frame's center, a pillow or folded blanket reads "Namaste," and another next to it, "Love"—upside-down from our perspective.[2] Governor Greg Abbott announced that recovery would take years and be far more extensive than the aftermath of Hurricane Katrina. And more expensive—Abbott estimated Texas might need more than $125 billion in aid.

Almost one year before Hurricane Harvey, the Supreme Court struck down Texas House Bill 2 (HB2) in *Whole Woman's Health v. Hellerstedt*. HB 2 had required that abortion clinics meet surgical-center requirements, which had forced twenty-two clinics to close—half of all the abortion clinics in Texas—after it passed in 2013. The regulations converted nine of the remaining nineteen into ambulatory surgical centers (ASC) that resemble hospitals with surgical bays, rather than non-ASC facilities, like Whole Woman's Health, which provide items like fleece blankets and tea to make patients more comfortable. ASCs are required to take medically unnecessary steps and treat patients as if they are undergoing major surgery with long-term recovery needs, which standard abortions do not require. Accordingly, patients must be transported in a wheelchair and stretcher, they cannot have herbal tea, and they must use "scratchy hospital blankets" because of "unnecessarily strict sterility standards."[3] Governor Abbott declared the Supreme Court ruling an attack on states' rights and an erosion of their authority to protect women's health and "innocent life." But the blanket tells a truer story than Texas' own leaders. It provides a sense of comfort and security in a charged setting that allows patients safe access to non–life-threatening procedures.[4] Justice Ginsburg asserted that "it is beyond rational belief that HB 2 could genuinely protect the health of women, and certain that the law would simply make it more difficult for them to obtain abortions."[5] Had HB 2 been upheld, more of these facilities would have been forced to close, and people would have had to travel long distances or engage in unsafe practices to terminate their pregnancies—all of which pose direct threats to their lives and sense of well-being.

At the center of these two narratives, the blanket bears witness to denial: the denial of climate change and global warming that will concoct new and ever-virulent weather patterns; the denial of comfort and security; the denial of the right to determine what happens to one's own body. Blankets witness our disasters. They fend off hypothermia, offer support and reassurance during crisis or distress, and provide warmth during the post-op chill. Their absence uncovers our vulnerabilities. With a blanket as witness, Sherman Alexie's (Spokane/Coeur d'Alene) story "War Dances" tells a narrative of colonial and familial histories, of healthcare and disease, of ceremony and healing.[6] Blankets become characters and carriers for the narrator, whose father is recovering from the amputation of half of his right foot and three toes from his left—an unfortunately common outcome for a serious diabetic. Disorientation and insecurity set in as the father lies exposed; "his decades of poor health and worse decisions were illuminated" on "white sheets in a white hallway under white lights." "I'm cold," he tells his son, who then sets out to look for another blanket. His request to a nurse elicits her irritation, but he reflects:

> After all, how many thousands of times had she been asked for an extra blanket? She was a nurse, an educated woman, not a damn housekeeper. And it was never really about an extra blanket, was it? No, when people asked for an extra blanket they were asking for a time machine. (33)

The blanket he carries back to his pale, chilled father is white and sterilized; it more closely resembles "the world's biggest coffee filter" than a blanket. Its own failure to be itself, the slip between form and content, exposes other blanket perceptions: The whiteness of the sheets, hallway, lights, and blanket create a scene of exposure, coldness, and sterility. Though the nurse "was neither compassionate nor callous," the blanket she provides does nothing to protect his father from the present. Through this unexpected exchange, the narrator reminds himself: In this setting, a stark hospital where people recover, decline, or die, patients and their loved ones most desire for the blanket to be a transportation object to another time, another dimension altogether—a *before* or *later*.

Rebekah Mannix, a pediatric emergency physician, writes of the ubiquitous blanket question: the moment when parents ask her for a blanket. She admits, "I was more than surprised when the only question parents asked me was the blanket question. In fact, I was mad. I must have thought my medical degree would or should exempt me from retrieving blankets.

Or that somehow the request belittled my hard-won status as an attending physician" (336). Mannix goes on to situate the blanket question as a gendered request, convinced that her male colleagues are never asked to provide this kind of care. Initially, she tried to fight back, to reply to the question with, "'I can see if your nurse can do that,' followed by some definitive pronouncement about testing or prognosis." As her career progressed, and as she also cared for her own children, and then for a sick husband, she "began to ask the questions that ambitious people sometimes forget to ask. 'Who do I want to be?' And so it came to pass that one day, I just got the blanket." Once she stopped fighting the question, the blanket became her ally. She began soliciting the request, and then soon learned to tuck her patients in; the extra time allows her to learn new and important things about her patients—maybe something medical, maybe just something about who they are when they aren't in a hospital bed.

The hospital blanket in "War Dances" illuminates the father's precarious state, the distance and isolation from his own body. He had once been "a large and dark man. Now he was just another pale, sick drone in a hallway of pale, sick drones" (34). But the son realizes that a "real blanket" will warm and comfort his father, and bring him back to someone more familiar—the person he is when he is not in a hospital bed. He wanders through the hospital, through the ER, the cancer, heart and vascular, neuroscience, orthopedic, women's health, pediatric, and surgical wards, and finally sees the person he's been looking for: another Native man.

Or, at least he assumes as much. They are in Seattle, after all, a global and diverse city, and so the man could also be Asian, the narrator concedes. Or he could be Mexican, "which is really a kind of Indian, too, but not the kind that I needed" (35). But his new friend turns out to be Lummi, and the two exchange a few jokes. His sister is in the delivery room, accompanied by their father performing a naming ceremony. His father has told the family this is a thousand-year-old tradition, but his son insists he "just made it up to impress himself. And the whole family goes along with it, even when we know it's bullshit. He's in the delivery room waving eagle feathers around. Jesus" (35–6). The story once again evokes time, the tension between "new" and "tradition," which calls their assumed distinctions into question. The naming ceremony is "supposed to protect the baby from all the technology and shit. Like hospitals are the big problem. You know how many babies died before we had good hospitals?" (36) The Lummi man defends the very space that the narrator has just presented as torturous, a system of failures. But he insists that his sister's baby needs no protection from new technology and hospitals, and his father's "traditional" ceremony is merely a performance.

Before his friend goes back to meet up with his family, the narrator asks him a favor: Does he have a good blanket to spare? He thought that if he found some Indians in the hospital, they would surely have a blanket, to which his friend replies: "That's fucking ridiculous. . . . And it's racist. . . . You're stereotyping your own damn people. . . . But damn if we don't have a room full of Pendleton blankets. New ones. Jesus, you'd think my sister was having, like, a dozen babies" (38). The phrase *Pendleton blankets* alone carries with it long and complicated histories that refuse to settle, or to allow for overly simplified notions of tradition and nostalgia, authenticity, or appropriation. The Pendleton Woolen Mills was originally established by white settlers, first by Thomas Kay, the "adventuresome young weaver" who had worked as a bobbin boy in Yorkshire mills before traveling by "boat, burro and buggy to settle in the new state of Oregon." He established Kay Woolen Mill in Salem in 1863, and then passed the business on to his daughter and her sons, who established a mill in Pendleton in 1896 (it officially opened in 1909) adjacent to the boundaries of the Umatilla reservation.[7] The Pendleton mill first made trade blankets and robes for Native and First Nations peoples. Weavers imitated designs and used colors reminiscent of Southwestern pottery, rugs, blankets, and robes, and then sold or traded back to Native people, whom the company refers to as its "first customers"—a decidedly capitalist take on settler and Native histories.[8]

But by the end of the nineteenth century, white settlers expressed their desires to play Indian or to possess indigeneity with their conspicuous consumption of Indian trade blankets. As described in a 1915 Pendleton catalog, tourists bought them to "take home as a souvenir of the Great West" (5). Pendleton bathrobes for men and women featured in this catalog were marketed as "the most beautiful creation in the way of an indoor garment that has ever been manufactured" to meet the "increasing demand of the white trade for something new and original and yet particularly suggestive of Western Life" (19). The catalog also describes various ways in which blankets came to be adapted to the desires of white consumerism, including domesticity and recreation: for use as "couch covers, bed covers, slumber robes, and for motoring, driving, canoeing, yachting, etc." (5). Pendletons transformed "other homely" necessities, like trunks, into seats of luxury.

In expensive coffee-table books with full-color photos, Pendletons and other Indian trade blankets are at once beautiful and captivating, but also suspended, like specimens behind glass. The histories and treatments of blankets as collectors' items, signifiers of class and white domesticity, do not account for what Pendleton blankets, trade blankets, robes, rugs, and hides mean in terms of affect, kinship, ceremony, inheritance, story—or why a woman about to give birth would have a "room full of Pendleton blankets," and what it means to give away a new Pendleton with a healing song. As Adrienne Keene (Cherokee) puts it, the relationship between Pendleton and Native communities is almost "symbiotic." Pendleton "saw a market in Native communities, and Native communities stepped up and bought, traded, and sold the blankets, incorporating them into 'traditional' cultural activities." Pendletons are presented at giveaways, and offered as gifts to commemorate a birth, death, marriage, or graduation. Although Pendleton capitalizes on appropriations of Native designs and cultures (see also its Portland Collection), Keene writes, "There's something just distinctly *Native* about Pendleton to me." Pendleton blankets have long been, and remain, a part of Native communities and identities, and Alexie captures this in a few sentences: "You're stereotyping your own damn people. . . . But damn if we don't have a room full of Pendleton blankets."

When the Lummi man emerges with his father and a new Pendleton blanket, the father declares his desire to sing a short healing song. And despite his own skepticism about his father's rituals, the son sings backup. The narrator maintains a certain skepticism and humor—he worries, for instance, that the honor song could last two minutes or two hours, and he notes how the old man cannot carry a tune. "Does a holy song lose its power if the singer is untalented?" But he accepts the song, and the blanket. And the old man reads his skeptical thoughts: "'It doesn't matter if you believe in the healing song,' he said. 'It only matters that the blanket heard'" (39). Alive and listening, the blankets in "War Dances" distill time and ambivalence; more precisely, they create a sense of time as itself ambivalent. The Pendleton suspends the chill, and for the time of the song—heard and carried by the blanket—father and son, sick and healthy, caregivers and patients, experience a kind of durational security.

Security refers both to a state of comfort—the feeling of safety—and to the forces or procedures assembled in safety's absence, against a body that threatens order and hierarchy. Textile artist Elizabeth Talford Scott's prayer shawl *Rocks in*

FIGURE 10 *Rocks in Prison* (1994) by Elizabeth Talford Scott.

Prison (1994) manages security's double edge. Atop a small quilted plane in blue and green floral print, Scott arranged small rocks and pebbles into rows in a snug grid. Battened down under red plastic mesh—the material used to bag onions or potatoes—the rows of rocks are aligned and bound into place with an embossed blue floss or filament that covers the rocks like a reinforced web. In each of the four corners rests a larger rock, held by the red mesh tied in a topknot.

Scott referred to *Rocks in Prison* not as a blanket or a quilt, but a *prayer*, according to George Ciscle, who curated the first retrospective of Scott's work and edited the accompanying catalog of her art and writing. Small yet astonishingly heavy, the piece lay draped across the backs or armrests of couches and chairs in her Baltimore home, which she shared with her daughter, multimedia artist Joyce Scott, for thirty-five years. *Rocks in Prison* waited at the ready to rest on a sore shoulder or back, to ease arthritic pain. As she offered or placed the prayer on a body, Scott often recited the Lord's Prayer. It was her way of healing, and she said she had arranged the lines of rocks as if they were text: "It's a prayer," she explained.[9]

> This is "in the beginning." In the beginning God created the heavens and the earth. Then the rocks. Created rocks all around then came man. No, animals and then man. And I think man is last. I don't know how many ifs or I's, amens I left out. (42)

Although Genesis 2 mentions gold and onyx, the rocks, minerals, and elements are typically not cited or remembered among the list and sequence of God's creations. Scott, however, places them before humans, and she makes no mention of an apple, just a rainbow:

> The blue would be the water or it could be clouds, a sign of the rainbow. See a rainbow doesn't just pop right yellow or gold, it's behind a cloud or something. It will bring all kinds of colors with it before it really turns into a rainbow. (42)

The blue, clouds, and rainbow—allusions to rain and order—may also evidence Scott's drawing on the traditions of ancestors. John Mbiti notes that in African religions, many "consider rocks and boulders to be dwelling places of spirits, the departed or the living dead" (55). Scott's concession, "I don't know how many ifs or I's, amens I left out," suggests doctrine and orthodoxy are not the point. It's the power of stones.

Elizabeth Talford Scott was from Chester, South Carolina, the daughter of sharecroppers who worked the same land on which her grandparents were enslaved. The stones refer to these ancestors too: formerly enslaved people and their descendants imprisoned in chain gangs, made to move and break rocks.[10] Scott warns of the dangers associated with treating rocks this way:

> They was bustin them and it exploded. So you see, you have to be so careful with a rock because that rock had probably been there for years and they were moving it. (42)

In keeping with rocks before men in her rendition of Christian teleology, and with the alluded-to power and sanctity of stones as spirits and guides, Scott foregrounds the rock's animacy and agency: The prisoner busts the rock, but the rock *explodes*. The rocks on Talford's blanket are at once trapped and secured—rocks in prison, and rocks as agents of prayer and healing. By merging rocks and blanket and mixing prayer with prison, Scott animates security's double entendre. *Rocks in Prison* suggests that blankets heal and help us feel secure; but they can also tell stories of terror and absence, of state secrets and sanctified violence.

Before President Obama left office, he denied Leonard Peltier's commutation. At this point, Peltier has spent forty years formally incarcerated by the settler nation. From his cell at Leavenworth in Kansas, he recorded his "soul thoughts, political musings and personal recollections" on scraps of paper. Among these, Peltier captures the blanket as a source of security, and a sign of one's humanity:

> Old-timers will tell you how they used to get thrown, buck naked in winter, into the steel-walled, steel-floored Hole without even so much as a cot or a blanket to keep them warm; they had to crouch on their knees and elbows to minimize contact with the warmth-draining steel floor. Today you generally get clothes and a cot and blanket— though not much else. (5)

Blankets, though indispensable companions, signify the absence of security in prison—not to have one, as Peltier suggests, is to be drawn to the threshold of nonlife. In such a precarious state, prisoners may turn the blanket or sheet into an agent of release.

Certain private medical and safety supply companies, such as American Detention Supplies, market anti-suicide blankets to prisons. Humane Restraint—which calls itself the "leading manufacturer of patient restraint systems and positioning aids that limit the ability of dangerous, combative, or unstable individuals to cause harm to themselves or staff members"—makes the Humane Safety Blanket, Smock, and Sleeping Bag, each of which provides "modesty and warmth," boasts material that sheds "soiling" and is "designed to resist use as a suicide implement."[11] Incongruously listed under the heading "Suicide Smocks and Suicide Blankets," these items are constructed to prevent suicides because they are impossible to tear—to end their lives, prisoners most commonly use bedding to hang themselves. Blankets, sleeping bags, smocks, and pillows seem ordinary until listed next to face shields, straitjackets (euphemistically called a "Humane Jacket"), hard-shell protective helmets, and a Humane Blanket Wrap, a "great transport aid" that resembles a whole-body straitjacket.

The blanket—the convolute, the shell—breaches the divisions between the internal and external world. This is its psychoanalytic function—to cover or shield a body from trauma. For the infant, a blanket is neither external nor internal, but a vital, vibrant, animated object that comes to have a life of its own, distinct from the human attached to it. Pediatrician and psychoanalyst D. W. Winnicott identifies blankets as *transitional objects*, the first *not-me* possession: "not part of the infant's body yet are not fully recognized as belonging to external reality" (3). Transitional phenomena, for Winnicott, have to do with the mouth and tactility: Complementing an auto-erotic experience (such as thumb-sucking), the baby might take an external object—like part of a sheet or blanket—along with the fingers. Or the baby plucks wool and collects it "to use it for the caressing part of the activity" (5). Parents come to understand the value of a transitional object: "The mother lets it get dirty and even smelly, knowing that by washing it she introduces a break in continuity in the infant's experience, a break that may destroy the meaning and value of the object to the infant" (5). Winnicott writes of the "special qualities" in the relationship between the infant and transitional object; the infant assumes rights over the object, and thus the object must never change unless changed by the infant. He adds that the object "must seem to the infant to give warmth, or to move, or to have texture, or to do something that seems to show it has vitality or reality of its own" (7). The blanket becomes lively, a child's animate companion.

Charles Schultz's *Peanuts* characters, including Linus and his blanket, were coincident with psychoanalytic discourse on transitional objects. Linus van Pelt is rarely seen without his blue security blanket, a transitional object from which he never transitions. Though he tries at times to give it up—and his symptoms resemble those of withdrawal from an addiction, anxiety, sweat, illness—and though he is sometimes ridiculed by Charlie or Lucy for carrying it, Linus always returns to his blanket. The term *Linus blanket* has come to stand for a security object, a pacifier, whether or not the object is an actual blanket. Project Linus, an organization whose volunteers (called *blanketeers*) make blankets for children "who are seriously ill, traumatized, or otherwise in need through the gifts of new, handmade blankets and afghans," features an iconic image of Linus holding his blanket against his cheek while sucking his thumb, and the motto "Providing Security Through Blankets."[12] Project Linus, which claims to have delivered nearly 6.5 million blankets since 1995, started the National Make a Blanket Day in 1999 after Eric Harris and Dylan Klebold murdered twelve of their classmates and one teacher at Columbine High School in Colorado. "We found that suddenly we were in need of a very large number of blankets, and quickly." Since then, Project Linus chapters hold an annual nationwide blanket bee.

In the wake of the 2012 Sandy Hook school shooting that killed twenty children and staff members, school shootings rose to an average of 1.37 times per week by 2014, when an Oklahoma-based company called ProTecht introduced a bulletproof blanket.[13] The Bodyguard Blanket, which resembles a rectangular pad—something you might expect a child to sleep on during a camping trip—is made of Dyneema, "the world's strongest fiber™."[14]

Five times stronger than Kevlar, Dyneema is used in ballistic helmets, vests, and inserts to protect soldiers, law enforcement officers, pilots, and "high-profile civilians," including children who attend public schools in the United States.[15] ProTecht tested the blanket at a shooting range and put it through the National Institute of Justice Series 3A Test, the same test used for police body armor. The blanket withstood the impact of a 12-gauge buckshot, 22-caliber, and 9-millimeter bullets.[16] Co-inventor Stan Schone explains in a televised news feature that in addition to the Dyneema, the quarter-inch-thick blanket contains an "impact gel"

FIGURE 11 Bodyguard Blanket.

made of soybean oil "that is the highest energy-absorbing material thus far known to mankind because of the sheer density of it."[17]

Steve Walker, one of the founders of ProTecht, adds that two tragedies inspired him to introduce the idea for the blanket, and then collaborate with Schone: the Sandy Hook shooting in 2012 and the 2013 tornadoes in Moore, Oklahoma, which killed twenty-four people. After Schone offers details about the blanket's materials, he explains, "It takes the bulle . . . the projectile is stopped by the Dyneema, and then part of the energy is dissipated through that, and then is further dissipated through the impact gel." Schone stops himself from fully uttering *bullet*, and opts instead for *projectile* and the passive voice. Throughout the interview, the two creators of the Bodyguard Blanket—decidedly *not* officially called the Bulletproof Blanket—talk their way carefully around the specters of violence directed at children.

Instead, to promote their product, Walker and Schone conjure images of children shot up with bullets or assaulted with debris by offering key details or Freudian slips without ever becoming too explicit. Schone plays to anxiety or grief by suggesting that if the kids killed in Oklahoma would have had these bright orange blankets, perhaps more could have survived the tornado: "It might have saved a life, it might not, but it might have saved one. It might have saved them all, we don't know." This object, he contends, gives kids "a better opportunity to survive." The Bodyguard Blanket is neoliberalism's answer to bodily security. Where life itself is an "opportunity," those willing to invest will have a better chance of survival. The "hard reality" of public schools, Walker explains, is that they cannot afford to construct tornado shelters. His answer to avoid raising taxes in communities like Edmond (where he works as a podiatrist) is for school districts to invest in Bodyguard Blankets—about $1,000 each, and easy to store until needed.

A two-minute video created to promote the Bodyguard Blanket performs an unintentional parody of post-9/11 terror.[18] The narrator cuts through a brief slideshow of stock images: a blur of white people walking, some holding briefcases; the back of a school bus; a voiceover that says,

"Just an ordinary day. Parents are going to work. Children are finding their seats in the classroom." The scene shifts to the interior of a classroom full of white children, with one African American child visible in the background. Again, all the images are stills, and the video runs like an amateur slideshow. The "dedicated teacher" prepares her students for a test, and we're reminded once more that this is "just an ordinary day," until a slide shifts to a close-up of an intercom on the ceiling. A man's urgent voice says, "Attention, attention! Teachers, this is not a drill. Prepare your students for a fully comprehen—" and the film cuts to moving images of disaster: the aftermath of tornadoes in Joplin, Missouri, an ambulance with audible sirens in Tuscaloosa, Alabama. When the montage comes to rest on an aerial view of Moore, Oklahoma, the narrator reports that students have endured tragedies of "all kinds." "Tornadoes have destroyed schools and caused the lives of boys and girls to end before they've hardly begun. Families have been overwhelmed with loss and sadness." Without pause, she continues, "And crazed gunmen have entered our schools prepared to kill our children and teachers." A white man appears, only half of his face visible in the field, and raises a gun to fill the other half, his index figure visible on the trigger, his expression sinister.

The video promotes the Bodyguard Blanket as a form of security against such "calamities" that leave "our children helpless and afraid." Both the video and the interview with the blanket's developers evoke a scene of children shot by bullets, using only suggestion or incomplete sentences and words. The product conceals itself as a form of capital by trafficking in terror, by conjuring a horrific imaginary. The design and materials filter down from the military and police to civilian lives; they offer a way for the public to avoid paying higher taxes for better infrastructure in public schools, and for Governor Abbott to pose with his rifles and tweet in October 2015, "I'm EMBARRASSED: Texas #2 in nation for new gun purchases, behind CALIFORNIA. Let's pick up the pace Texans. @NRA."[19] Abbott's tweet followed a shooting at Umpqua Community College in Roseburg, Oregon, earlier that month, where ten people were shot and killed, and the murders of nine parishioners at the Emanuel AME Church in Charleston, South Carolina, in June—to cite just two. Mass shootings in the United States reached a record high in 2015: They happened almost every day, and often more than once a day.[20]

But most high-tech blankets are geared toward a more elemental survival: they focus on heat. Blizzard Blanket, the mylar Space Blanket, and Heatsheets are marketed to outdoor enthusiasts, backcountry hikers, and marathon runners at the finish line. After the bomb explosions at the 2013 Boston Marathon, a photographer captured a pile of unused Heatsheets, a tangle of clean debris with corporate logos visible: Adidas, the investment firm John Hancock, the Boston Athletic Association.[21] The image stands in stark contrast to other photos that memorialize the explosions with blood, glass and other forms of shrapnel, indiscernible belongings strewn on the sidewalks and streets. Some runners wrapped themselves in Heatsheets to regulate their body temperatures, but also to provide a measure of comfort and safety in the maelstrom. The visual archive from the Boston Marathon bombings makes evident the blanket as a flexible object—they regulate body temperature, stanch bleeding, carry or cover a wounded body. They embrace a person in shock.

UNFOLD 5

Hospital blankets must be white so they can be bleached over and over again. They partially cover tubes, machines, bags, an ailing body. These blankets are thin, and their whiteness a kind of dare. Every time I visit someone in the hospital, I stare at the blanket and scan for stains. When I find one, I wonder what kind of tragedy or trauma couldn't be bleached out of its warp and weft.

I don't at all remember being in Kevin's hospital room, or even seeing him, on that trip to Denver when I stayed in the Ronald McDonald House. But I do remember playing pool in the hospital with my dad. I wore my light turquoise suit—matching pants and button-down shirt—and couldn't wait to show off my new skills. I racked, Dad broke. Or maybe he let me break. I made a few good shots. But the pool table was smaller than what I was used to. The felt was coarser, or just newer. And it was probably level; I was accustomed to working with a slope. The pockets had leather nets to catch the balls, but I preferred my grandparents' table where the ball traveled down a dark inner tunnel, gathering momentum until it reached its destination and clanked with comrades. As we played, I noticed the room's smell, antiseptic and sick. And then a girl around my age appeared to watch us. She had no hair and wore a hospital gown. Dad made some sort of overture to her, assuming she maybe wanted to play with us or take his place. His invitation felt like a betrayal, or the deepest form of rejection. I suddenly felt like a caricature— every feature, including that turquoise suit and my mullet, was noticeable, exaggerated. After that, I aspired to be camouflage—present but definably inconspicuous.

If blankets are time machines, how long will a blanket hold a person's scent, to allow that moment of plunging face into fold to transport back in time?

When Kevin went into remission for one year, he played tennis, took up fishing, and worked at the local record store. He bought me my first stereo, a deep red JVC with detachable speakers. I used it to record my own "radio shows" because it also had a dual tape deck—I could play music and record at the same time. He bought me the new Tears for Fears tape, *Songs from the Big Chair*. Because Kevin loved Prince and the Revolution and parachute pants, I wore purple parachute pants. I don't remember when or how this all ended; I only remember that he guided me, and I've needed him ever since.

When Edwidge Danticat's mother was diagnosed with cancer, her nurse explained that cancer isn't always a *mass*, "but how it's sometimes like a blanket over organs, or like chains that trap them, and how cancer can't always be cut out but at times only minimally reduced" (138). Kevin's cancer was a like a blanket that trapped us. It covered our family, enveloped us. I hid in one of its folds. His nurse held me on her lap at his deathbed, and whispered to me about his last breaths. He had been saying something, caught mid-sentence by death. I don't know what he was trying to say.

5 COVER

To write about blankets is to be lured to metaphor and cliché. *Patchwork, weave, unravel, unfold, stitch. A blanket of snow. A blanket of stars. Blanket statement. Blanket policy. To pull the wool over one's eyes. A wolf in sheep's clothing.* Good metaphors are rich with tension, precise yet expansive, *lively* because they provoke surprise—the reader or listener expected something different.[1] The blanket is a pliable object, an unruly form until one folds it—into shape, into language. The blanket beckons our imagination, our capacity to narrate war and trauma, shootings and bombings, pleasure, birth, death, security, virality, rocks, copper, gypsum, marble, and concrete. *The fabric of time*—not just a nice metaphor—refers to making a plane. A *fabrication* can signify an invention or creation, as in a lie or deceit, or as in the construction of an object, often with metal and stone. *Fabricate* and *fabric* both derive from the Latin *fabrica*, which refers to art or craft, the manner of construction, or even skillful production. *Fabrica* is derived from *faber*, forger or smith. Like *to forge, to fabricate* has the double valence of creativity and deception. When magicians perform a trick, they might conceal the scene—a specific object, a table, or their own hand—with a blanket, a cover. The audience watches with anticipation as something underneath and out of sight transpires, and then transforms for the reveal, the magic. As covers, blankets keep our secrets and reserve our grief and pleasures. They are narrative ciphers. Mnemonic devices.

President Obama fulfilled his goal to visit all fifty states during his presidency when in May 2015, he traveled to South Dakota, the last state on his list, and delivered the commencement address to the Lake Area Technical Institute in Watertown. The school commissioned Dakota artist and citizen of the Sisseton-Wahpeton Oyate DeVon Bursheim to make a star quilt to present to Obama.[2] Star quilts are cherished gifts to honor and protect the recipient on a journey: memorial feasts, celebrations, naming ceremonies, marriages, powwows, and basketball tournaments. The owíŋža (quilt) signifies recognition and respect, and it is made to be given away. Most star quilts feature a single eight-sided star in the center, made up of small diamond-shaped patches conjoined in eight sections. The star pattern is reminiscent of early buffalo robe designs, and the quilt a distant echo of the robe—star quilts are the symbolic replacement of buffalo robes, according to Richard Peterson. The near-extermination of bison by settlers in the mid- to late nineteenth century coincided with the incarceration of Oceti Sakowin children in mission and boarding schools, where they learned quilting. While some textile histories attribute the quilt's design to the "Variable Star" pattern used in mid-seventeenth-century

New England, according to Oceti Sakowin cosmology, the star represents the morning star, a guiding light.

At the time of Obama's visit, the Keystone XL (KXL) pipeline was awaiting his final approval. The $8 billion, 1,179-mile TransCanada pipeline would pass through Alberta, Saskatchewan, Montana, South Dakota, and Nebraska: homelands of the Blackfoot, Lakota, Dakota, Assiniboine, Ponca, Cree, and Dene peoples. And while much attention was given to the fight against KXL for the unlikely alliances it created, the tar sands, pipelines, fracking, and other forms of extractivism are not only "universal" issues, but specifically matters of Native/Indigenous/First Nations sovereignty and land rights.[3] Cree, Dene, and Métis communities have been on the front lines against the Alberta tar sands and TransCanada for years. In September 2010, the Assembly of First Nations of Canada asked the US government to account for the environmental impact of the tar sands, including the high rate of cancer downstream in the Fort Chipewyan community. The next year, the Mother Earth Accord, signed by the Oceti Sakowin and other tribal nations and organizations, was presented to President Obama at the 2011 White House Tribal Nations Conference. The document exhorts Obama and Secretary of State John Kerry to reject the permit for the KXL pipeline and to reduce reliance on oil, including the tar sands. The Mother Earth Accord also asserts that "Indigenous people are most vulnerable to the social, cultural, spiritual, and environmental impacts of climate change."[4]

As she handed her quilt to President Obama, DeVon Bursheim said, "Tasina Pezuta Win emakiyapi ye," *they call me blanket woman*. Unbeknownst to the Lake Area Technical Institute and Obama staffers, Bursheim had sewn a subtle but still quite visible "NOKXL" on the back of the quilt. Bursheim prayed for her land and water in the giveaway. In November 2015, Obama rejected the permit for KXL. As Tom Goldtooth of the Indigenous Environmental Network put it, Obama's rejection of the KXL helped Cree and Dene people at the source come one step closer to shutting down the tar sands and defeating the black snake.[5] But just days after officially assuming the US presidency, Donald Trump signed executive actions to allow for the construction of KXL; and one week before Nebraska's Public Service Commission was set to determine KXL's specific route from Canada to Nebraska, TransCanada's Keystone pipeline leaked well over 200,000 gallons (or 5,000 barrels) of oil in South Dakota. Most reports of the leak identified its location as being on "private land" near the small town of Amherst. But the oil also infiltrated the soil and ground water near the Lake Traverse Reservation, home of the Sisseton-Wahpeton Oyate.

Trump's executive order in January 2017 also approved the completion of the Dakota Access Pipeline, owned by Houston-based Energy Transfer Partners: a $3.8 billion, 1,110-mile fracked-oil pipeline from the Bakken shale fields in North Dakota to Peoria, Illinois. The plans for the pipeline included nine major intersections between the pipeline and rivers in present-day North Dakota, South Dakota, and Iowa. The pipeline poses risks for multiple populations along its route, from spills and leaking that will occur to the introduction of invasive species, fungi, and microbes transported by drilling equipment. People who live on reservations proximate to the pipeline are disproportionately at risk, including citizens of the Standing Rock Sioux Tribe whose lands straddle present-day South and North Dakota.[6] In 2014, a year before his trip to South Dakota, President Obama visited the Standing Rock Sioux Nation—his first visit to a reservation as president, and the first-ever presidential visit to a North Dakota reservation. As a candidate in 2008, Obama had been adopted by the Crow Nation and given the name *Barack Black Eagle*, One Who Helps the People Across the Land, and his time at Standing Rock in 2014 gestured back to the promises and commitments he made to Indian Country when he was on the campaign trail: education reform, economic development, the "respect" of tribal sovereignty, and the recognition of tribal jurisdiction for major crimes. Standing Rock chairman Dave Archambault II and councilmember Frank Whitebull presented Obama with a red, white, and blue star quilt.

In April 2016, water protectors from the Oceti Sakowin founded the Sacred Stone Camp at the confluence of Mni Sose and the Cannonball River.[7] Despite statements from the Standing Rock Sioux Tribe and the Tribal Historic Preservation Office that the completion of the Dakota

Access Pipeline would damage historic preservation areas, the Army Corps of Engineers fast-tracked a permit to finish the construction, citing "no direct or indirect impacts."[8] By August, water protectors had established three additional camps and were deeply engaged in peaceful and prayerful protection of their relatives, human and nonhuman, threatened by the completion of the pipeline. At the main camp, Oceti Oyate, Native and non-Native water protectors and allies arrived daily with supplies, including blankets and food, to share. While the Obama administration remained at first silent, and later suggested they would let the situation "play out" for several more weeks, water protectors declared their determination to remain in camp and to stop the final construction of the pipeline. The final section to be completed would lurk within one mile of Standing Rock Sioux Tribe's lands, across Mni Sose and under Lake Oahe—two significant water sources for the tribe and for millions of people downriver. *Playing out* included attack dogs, pepper spray, water cannons, concussion grenades, Blackwater surveillance tactics, helicopters, tanks, private security forces, North Dakota state police, police from neighboring states, arrests that sometimes took water protectors out of state without any method of contact with people who could free them from custody, elder abuse, the defamation of sacred bundles and *inipi,* and illegal construction.

In September, and certainly in October and November, temperatures in North Dakota can dip below freezing at night. But water protectors were undeterred. With supplies, including blankets and cordwood, water protectors were prepared and emboldened to stay in camp, to keep fire, through the winter. While they endured floodlights, helicopters, and people sneaking into camp under cover (posing as allies, but later reporting lies to ignite highly flammable racism in Mandan and Bismarck), a monument called *Dignity* was dedicated at the Lewis and Clark rest area near Chamberlain, South Dakota, on the homelands of the Kul Wicasa Oyate, the Lower Brule Sioux. The 50-foot, 11-ton statue stands on a ridge above Mni Sose, downriver from Oceti Oyate and the other Standing Rock camps. Artist Laureate of South Dakota Dale Lamphere designed the figure to honor Lakota and Dakota people. He used three Native women models, ages 14, 29, and 55, to fabricate the face of the Native woman who stands with her arms outstretched, a star quilt across her back. The stars on the quilt are composed of more than 100 four-foot, blue, stainless steel diamonds that flutter when the wind passes through. A central stainless steel pipe bears the weight of the quilt "and the fabricated sculpture of the woman."[9] Her dress is patterned after a two-hide dress from the 1850s.

Proximity to the monument and its fluttering star quilt evokes a kind of awe at Lamphere's design and engineering. But *Dignity* cannot bear the weight of colonial history, installed as it is at a rest area named for Lewis and Clark, who were sent on a trespass mission following the Louisiana

Purchase, the largest real estate "deal" in US history. Nick Estes puts the Louisiana Purchase into context:

> None of the Native Nations west of the Mississippi consented to the sale of their lands to a sovereign they neither recognized nor viewed as superior. It was only after we rebuffed Lewis and Clark for failing to pay tribute for their passage on our river [Mni Sose] that they labeled the Oceti Sakowin "the vilest miscreants of the savage race." ("Fighting")

Dignity was commissioned by a private citizen from Rapid City, a gift to "all the people of South Dakota," on the occasion of the 125th anniversary of statehood. South Dakota became a state in November 1889—just months after Congress passed an act which yet again reduced the once-vast land base of the Oceti Sakowin, and divided the nation into smaller reservations, including Standing Rock, Pine Ridge, Cheyenne River, and Lower Brule. Although *Dignity* was offered as a monument to honor Lakota and Dakota people, its site on the upper banks of Mni Sose—not only a water source, but a relative to the Oceti Sakowin—reads more like degradation under cover. A pipeline, which defames *Dakota*—the term for *friend* or *ally*—was also commissioned along this river. It will leak, and its concrete shell will fail to shield Mni Sose and surrounding lands from the traumas of extractivism.

Dignity, cast and permanent, inadvertently honors an ongoing deception. But DeVon Bursheim's "NOKXL" fulfills

FIGURE 12 *Placeholder* (2017) by Marie Watt.

the form of the gift and exchange—the star quilt honors the recipient, and the message it bears honors the sovereignty, self-respect, and determination of Dakota and Lakota people. Like sovereignty, *dignity* is not something that can be gifted or bestowed.

Contemporary artist Marie Watt's (Seneca) *Placeholder* (2017) stages the limits of a monument against the potential of a blanket. On a 56 × 140-inch, bright green reclaimed wool blanket, Watt embroidered the phrase *ephemeral monument* in transparent glass Czech seed beads. The reclaimed wool comes from a four-point trade blanket, perhaps a nineteenth-century trade blanket manufactured by the Hudson's Bay Company.[10] Four-point blankets feature four bands that cross the width of the blanket. The blanket points on *Placeholder* are black, a rich contrast to its green expanse.

Watt borrowed the phrase *ephemeral monument* from John N. Low's discussion of parade floats in the 1893 Chicago World's Fair, which featured Simon Pokagon (Potawatomi) and other living Native people as monuments—animated displays of arrested time. And yet, Low argues, "the Potawatomi also promoted and participated in more ephemeral monuments and living memorials, such as the rhetoric of land claims, and the spectacles of encampments, parades, speeches, canoeing, etc., that not only entertained the Chicago public but also maintained the ties of the Pokagon Potawatomi to their Chicago" (xiv). Although not fabricated in steel, granite, bronze, or marble, land claims, camps, and messages to the president of the United States sewn into a blanket are monumental acts. Watt, too, honors the blanket by turning it into a monument with a message about time and embodiment: the blanket itself a portable accumulation of time—the fur trade, forced movement, long winters—and a companion, shell, layer, and protector around bodies who have been persistently deemed ephemeral, always disappearing. Watt cannot be sure of the blanket's provenance, though this is of course part of *Placeholder*'s argument. The blanket is just that, a placeholder, to denote the ephemeral: stories and histories unknown to some, but rendered in the collective memory and storied inheritance of others.

When Jacqueline Tobin, a journalist from Colorado, came to Charleston, South Carolina, in 1994 to research handmade grass baskets, she encountered Ozella McDaniel Williams in the City Market, where she sold her handmade quilts. Williams unrolled one of her quilts and asked Tobin, "Did you know that quilts were used by slaves to communicate on the Underground Railroad?" (17) That question would lead Tobin on a three-year research process that culminated in a co-authored study of quilt codes, or the Underground Railroad Code, as Tobin and her co-author Dr. Raymond G. Dobard refer to it in their 2000 book *Hidden in Plain View*. The authors make clear that the book is an account of one family's involvement with, and knowledge of, quilt codes. In other words, this study is at its heart the account of Ozella McDaniel Williams, her inheritance of story, a knowledge of quilts and patterns dominant in African American quilting, and her passing on a familial memory of the secrets and metaphors carried by quilts.

Williams identified ten different codes, each with distinct patterns. They were used both to signal preparation for escape and to indicate directions on the journey. In this sense, the quilts were code and metaphor, since metaphors are themselves a kind of transport, which "is why a metaphor is said to have a 'vehicle'" (Stockton 92). As signs and metaphors, the quilt patterns instructed enslaved people on how to prepare for escape, and where to go—the patterns and stitching a topography (*Hiding* 71). Tobin and Dobard, who is a professor of art history at Howard and a quilt maker himself, also researched "African cultural antecedents and American quilt making precedents" to make connections to the Underground Railroad Quilt story-code (27). The quilt patterns worked in conjunction with spirituals, carried by collective memory.

Hidden in Plain View foregrounds African American quilting as a genre that evokes Joseph Roach's concept of *surrogation*: a process that does not begin or end, but instead refers to the process a community undertakes to survive. Quilting is a diasporic cultural production, an encoding of West and Central Africa, the Caribbean, and US port cities where enslaved people were forced to migrate. Tobin and Dobard's study shows that enslaved Africans and their descendants were "not hapless individuals, but ones who remembered or were taught their past, and through the materials available began to reconstruct themselves in the United States, a new very restricted environment" (5). With Williams's stories at the center of their study, Tobin and Dobard make clear that although the quilt appears to be an everyday bedcover, it functions as a mnemonic device. That is, as a necessary, but ordinary and familiar object, the quilt provided the perfect cover: "Communicating secrets using ordinary objects is very much a part of African culture . . . . Messages can be skillfully passed on through objects that are seen so often they become invisible" (35). And, because quilts needed to be placed outside to air out, quilt codes could be posted without drawing attention.

Tobin and Dobard's book received a great deal of press, and soon, elementary school curricula, projects, and field trips were devoted to the quilt code.[11] But the book also received notable critiques about its veracity. Because Ozella Williams is the only person known to have identified and decoded an elaborate system—no others have come forward to corroborate her claims, and no written documents have been found—some critics of the study claim that Williams may have fabricated the code. No one seems to deny that her oral history is compelling, and that her engagement with Jacqueline Tobin is in and of itself intriguing.[12]

In 2001, then director of the New Jersey Historical Commission's African American history program Giles R. Wright issued a detailed critique of *Hidden in Plain View* and became one of the book's most outspoken skeptics. Wright's concerns ranged from the book's lack of corroborative evidence and several factual errors, to its hand in adding to the mythologies of the Underground Railroad. For instance, he argued that given the elaborate code system presented by Williams, the book implies a large number of enslaved people participated in the Underground Railroad system. But the "overall number of Underground Railroad runaways was very small, a tiny fraction" of the total enslaved population.[13] Wright is careful to point out that his critique is not based on the lack of *written* evidence, but on these other factors, including the singularity of Williams's narrative. Both the critiques and admiration for Tobin and Dobard's work endure, and some, such as quilt historian Laurel Horton, are less interested in debunking the code than on exploring why the story persists.[14]

Joseph Roach argues that collective memory catalyzes surrogation, and because collective memory is always uneven and imaginative, surrogation almost always "fails"— it creates deficits and surplus. Surrogation may also incite phobic anxieties (2). To frame Williams's request of Tobin to *write this down*, and even her memories themselves, as "circum-Atlantic performance" is to release both Williams and *Hidden in Plain View* from a potentially phobic search for origin and evidence. *Performance* in this sense draws on the idea of expressive movements as reserves: haptic memories, the patterned movements made and remembered by bodies, residual movements in images, words, or silence, and the imaginary movements of dreams (Roach 26).

Perhaps the Underground Railroad Code was taken too literally and schematically by Tobin and Dobard, perhaps not. Nevertheless, the collective knowledge, surrogate memories, and imaginings of dangerous escapes and migrations north most certainly made their way into quilts. As Hannah Rosen puts it, quilts "allowed enslaved people to communicate, under the radar of enslavers." Belief in the possibility that "there was a way out, even if treacherous . . . helped shape a culture of resistance that allowed enslaved people to flee in the thousands when the opportunity was presented, either by individual circumstances or when the Civil War broke out." And scholars, quilt historians, and artists (some of whom occupy all three identities) have continued to study, make, and draw on the traditions of African American quilting, including the mythologies related to quilt code.[15]

Algernon Miller interpreted quilt code for his winning design for Frederick Douglass Circle in Harlem. His original plans included a large-scale granite quilt to feature quilt code, and a granite curbstone perimeter arranged to create a sunburst effect at the approximate spot of the North Star. As he described, the pie-shaped pattern would create a sunburst effect on the perimeter of the granite quilt.[16] Some historians—including David Blight, a Frederick Douglass biographer and scholar—brought their concerns about *Hidden in Plain View* to the fore. Blight (and others) reasoned that Douglass's own writings contain no evidence for quilt code, which makes dubious the association of the code with his memorial.

Though Miller and others defended his vision as *art*, distinct from verifiable history, the final installation (completed in 2009) includes a modified round geometric pattern made of granite, without specific attribution to quilt code.[17] As the New York City Department of Cultural Affairs describes it, the design is "based on traditional African-American quilt motifs, as well as a bronze perimeter fence inspired by the form of a wagon wheel. The centerpiece of the site is the water wall depicting the Big Dipper constellation and the North Star."[18] While granite is a practical, durable material for an outdoor sculpture and memorial, Miller's plan to use it as the quilt's fabric also binds geologic time to the rich histories of quilting, and the quilt's potential to guide people to safety, to free them from enslavement.

Quilters and artists such as Patty Elwin Davis and Elizabeth Talford Scott also pass on the histories, memories, and surrogations of codes and stars in their work. Davis's 65 × 65-inch quilt, *"Live Free or Die": Harriet Tubman and the Secret Codes of the Underground Railroad* (2004) depicts Harriet Tubman at the center, holding a shotgun—the stock side of the gun rests on a green landscape covered with flowers and large stones.[19] The quilt's far-right border features constellations, including the North Star; and in a smaller frame to the left, three people navigate a swamp or stream, at night, as they make their way north and use the stars as a guide. Panels of quilt code—like North Star, Monkey Wrench, Crossroads, Flying Geese, and Drunkard's Path—frame the top and left sides of the quilt. Scott's *The Plantation Quilt* (1979–80) places, in her own words, "the mother of the stars in the center. That's the dipper of the sky" (Ciscle 29). The quilt approximates the view of a clear night sky in South Carolina from the vantage point of a porch on which women would sit to sew after all-day field labor. The stitching on the stars represents the planted rows of crops. *The Plantation Quilt* sutures familial memories of enslavement, and Scott's own memories of working in cotton fields as a sharecropper's daughter, with the deep time and guiding light of the stars. Stars blanket the sky, and make their way into code and cover.

Despite their distinct practices, histories, spiritual and aesthetic traditions, artists like DeVon Bursheim, Ozella McDaniel Williams, Elizabeth Talford Scott, Patty Elwin

Davis, and so many others use blankets to intervene in dominant discourse, and to create their own narratives with materials available and familiar. For quilt makers, the blanket becomes a surrogate medium: a carrier of family stories and collective memories, histories unspoken or unremarked, of secrets and codes. The blanket is a political act and a companion. Scott started quilting again after her daughter Joyce went to Mexico to earn her MFA. Quilting, she said, filled "empty moments" and kept her "from getting so lonely" (13). To quilt is to make a memory, a proxy to fill the absence. To quilt is to summon the spirits and guides, the ghosts, and the absent love.

UNFOLD 6

I lived with ghosts—not a metaphor, I mean apparitions, the dead who make themselves animate again—long before Kevin died. They were especially active in my room upstairs, which was between Kevin's room and a door to the attic. They found me every night, but only if I was alone. A blanket played an essential role in both of my methods of survival, the first preferable to the second: I would start in bed, and then—as soon as everyone else was asleep—sneak out with a pillow and blanket and make camp on the floor of someone else's room. I learned how to appease squeaky doors, and not to site myself in the pathway from a bed to a bathroom, lest I be discovered. The second tactic was to hide under the covers all night, with strategically placed air vents, in my own bed.

I imagine this period as the formation or sedimentation of my queerness. On the surface, this was a house that my siblings and I *grew up in*, at least three of the four of us. It was the backdrop to the disciplining functions of normativity. But inside of all this, under cover, I formed a secret self. I grew sideways, as in, I dwelled in what Kathryn Bond Stockton calls the "moving suspensions and shadows of growth." Stockton likens sideways growth to the death drive, "something that locates energy, pleasure, vitality, and (e)motion in the back-and-forth of connections, and extensions that are not reproductive" (13). Though I would have preferred not to see the ghosts, they were companionable enough. But my attachment to the house was downright libidinal. And I could not have lived without my dog, Josh, who endured my persistent overtures. He even complied when I invited him to join me for a warm bath. He was the only friend I had, so he was on the hook for every plan I made. He sat through the tea parties I threw for him, front paws at the edge of the green and white-checkered blanket I spread in the living room.

The dog is a living, growing metaphor for the child's strangeness, a "companion in queerness," a "figure for the child beside itself, engaged in a growing quite aside from growing up," writes Stockton (90). She reads David, the protagonists' dog in Radclyffe Hall's *The Well of Loneliness* (1928), as a figure for what it means to be beside oneself with sorrow (101). But Josh—absent David's messianic allusions, but a complementary 1980s name nonetheless—was more than a vehicle, a metaphor; he was himself a carrier for grief. A few months after Kevin died, Josh walked in front of a moving car, with apparent purpose and intent. I didn't witness it, and I remember nothing but flashes of my mom's panic, who saw it all just seconds too late to intervene. Even with all of his canine intuition, with his drive to love and care for us all, the dog chose a return of sorts. My family has talked little of it since, except for the quiet surrender of knowing that he, too, couldn't accept the permanent absence of the person he loved.

6 CARRIERS

Marie Watt's *Blanket Stories* installations feature folded and stacked new, reclaimed, and donated blankets.[1] Often arranged in columns of variable height, resting on cedar, fir, or stone plinths, *Blanket Stories* resemble and evoke the shape and stature of monumental forms, memorials, and monoliths. But they also conjure the shape and scale of totem poles made by Indigenous peoples of the Pacific Northwest coast, and the region's conifer trees with which Watt grew up (43).

Blanket Stories: Seven Generations, Adawe, Hearth (2013), a stunning 36-foot column, radiates a monumental aura. Its scale recalls ancient structures and monuments to empire, such as Trajan's Column (a reference point for Watt), a memorial to Trajan's defeat of the Dacians in back-to-back wars fought between AD 101 and 106. Symbols of precious victories and monuments to colonialism and empire are typically made with venerable materials, such as marble, granite, and bronze; Trajan's Column features fine Luna marble from Carrara and a bronze statue of St. Peter (added in 1588). Watt's column, composed of wool blankets

FIGURE 13 *Blanket Stories: Seven Generations, Adawe, Hearth* (2013) by Marie Watt.

and stacked on a cedar base, arrests monumentality for the blanket, a transportation object and carrier of stories. The title refers to time and inheritance (*Seven Generations*); place (*Adawe*, or Ottawa, its site in the National Gallery of Canada); and home (*Hearth*, a space of warmth and fire).

Tags attached to some of the blankets denote materially the presence of those who contributed a blanket, and a story, to the installation. Watt reflects:

> Blankets are everyday objects. We take them for granted, yet as we use them, they quietly record our histories: a lumpy shape, a worn binding, mended patches. Every blanket holds a story. In the secondhand and thrift-store blankets I use in much of my work, I can only guess at the story. But when I can work with contributed blankets, I ask each contributor to record the blanket's story (or the contributor's story as it relates to the blanket) on a tag. These stories remain with the blankets in their installations, and are also transcribed and collected, so that others can share them.[2]

For years, Watt collected blankets. From thrift stores and giveaways, she stockpiled blankets with a sense that they were necessary to archive, even without an authenticating story attached. Now, through her art, the blanket would receive a new story, a new life. Initially, she set out to make one piece: two wool panels covered in hand-sewn patterns cut out of blankets.[3] But that project was too much for her to do alone, so she invited loved ones, family, friends, and the community to contribute. Watt created a new kind of quilting bee; as people worked on the blankets, they told more stories. Each new stitch—some made by experts, others by tentative hands—created its own time signature. The acts of sewing and stitching, stacking and cleaning, also archive the secrets, honor the dead, and mark the transformation of a community.

Some *Blanket Stories*—such as *Cousin Rose, Four Pelts, Sky Woman and Relations* (2004)—are topological marvels whose twists and curves resemble Möbius strips.

FIGURE 14 *Blanket Stories: Cousin Rose, Four Pelts, Sky Woman and Relations* (2004) by Marie Watt.

During a visit to Watt's studio in Portland, Oregon, I could not resist the question that surely everyone asks: How do these stacks of folded blankets not topple over? "Do you really want to know?" Watt said. "No, I guess not. Or, maybe." But I chose not to write down the explanation or commit it to memory. I opt instead for *magic*.

The cast bronze blankets in *Blanket Stories: Transportation Object, Generous Ones, Trek* (2014), an 18 × 4 × 6-foot sculpture permanently installed at the Tacoma Art Museum, tower and curve into an *X*, but do not touch or meet one another—their only points of contact are the ground and the building itself. As Watt explains, the X is a signature, a term of endearment, the indicator of a name on a treaty, the mark of a place or event.[4] If the forms were to continue into the museum itself—if we could follow them through the walls, the museum space and back into the ground—they would form two concentric O shapes. But we can only imagine such continuity. Bronze is a practical material for this outdoor sculpture, but Watt also uses the form for its historical resonance: Bronze is used to make "busts of statesmen and military leaders." These stacked bronze blankets are keepers of memories, markers of beginnings and endings, of security and scarcity. That is, while the blanket may at first seem ordinary and even forgettable, Watt's installations remind us that blankets, too, are monumental: They carry histories of colonization; they witness and cover death; they protect and provide security; they are memorials to dispossession. They are also witnesses to survivance, and to moments of "ecstatic giving."

FIGURE 15 *Witness* (2015) by Marie Watt.

Embroidered outlines of a Kwakaka'wakw (First Nations peoples of Vancouver Island) potlatch cover *Witness* (2015), a 71 × 180.5-inch reclaimed Hudson's Bay Point blanket. For Coast Salish people of the Pacific Northwest coast of Canada and the United States, Bill Kte'pi explains, a potlatch is a gift-giving ceremony or festival. "In the potlatch system, social status is determined not by wealth per se but by the capacity to give wealth away" (1741). Wool blankets were a common unit by which wealth was measured, and even the value of coins was set according to the number of blankets for which one could be exchanged. Watt adapted the scene on *Witness* from a photo of a 1913 potlatch, "Quamichan Potlatch, Coast Salish, 1913," taken by Reverend C. M. Tate.[5] In the photo, people stand with their backs to the camera; many wear shawls and blankets. They focus their attention on two people who stand on the roof of a longhouse, tossing blankets down to the crowd. Reverend Tate has captured one blanket in mid-air, just before it will land on the hands raised to meet it. As Watt notes, this potlatch would have been an act of civil disobedience in 1913, because the Canadian and US governments declared the potlatch system illegal from 1885 to the 1950s. "Not only did the government disapprove of Indigenous people gathering: giving away one's wealth was considered backwards and wasteful." The act conflicted with Euro-American acquisitive values. The embroidered community fills the blanket's frame in *Witness*, along with a stack of blankets in the far-right corner. And next to this stack, Watt stitched an outline of herself holding her daughter, whose face is the only one we see. "I have come to think of blankets as transportation objects, both physically and metaphorically," Watt explains. She and her daughter join the community, across space and time, and become witness to and participants in an ongoing practice.

Watt transforms blankets into lively agents and media, even when they are at rest and waiting in her studio. The quiet piles of blankets come alive, again, in her structures of narrative and memory, even in the choice of material itself. In the case of *Witness*, the Hudson's Bay Company Point Blanket onto which Watt stitches a potlatch and community is an icon of colonial capitalism. In 1670, King Charles II granted the Royal Charter for the Hudson's Bay Company. The document claims exclusive trading rights in the entire Hudson Bay basin for "the Governor and Company of Adventurers." Charles also named his cousin Prince Rupert the first governor of the territory, "henceforth known as 'Rupert's Land.'" From 1670 to 1870, the Hudson's Bay

Company assumed exclusive right to trade in and colonize a vast region that contains the rivers that flow into Hudson Bay and their entire drainage area: present-day northern Québec and Labrador, northern and western Ontario, all of Manitoba, most of Saskatchewan, south and central Alberta, and parts of the Northwest Territories and Nunavut. Hudson's Bay Company established forts and trading routes, and Cree, Assiniboine, Métis, and other First Nations peoples traded and supplied the Company with furs. Nevertheless, the Royal Charter treated the lands as *terra nullius*, no one's land; Hudson's Bay Company had no regard for the sovereignty of First Nations peoples in this expansive territory. The coat of arms for this "Company of Adventurers" featured four beavers with the words *Pro Pelle Cutem*—roughly translated, "for furs we risk our hides" (Tichenor 9).

The famous striped Hudson's Bay Company Point Blanket, produced by Witney Mills in Oxfordshire, England, beginning in the late 1600s, became an icon and currency of the fur trade.[6] Weavers initially devised the point system to indicate the intended size of a finished blanket. Since tariffs were paid by the blanket, blankets would be cut to size *after* import (a four-point blanket could be cut in half to make two two-point blankets, for instance) to avoid higher tariffs. And as with Pendleton blankets, Hudson's Bay Company blankets became essential and flexible objects for Indigenous peoples. They often wore the blankets as robes, but also used them as covers, sails, and objects for burial and birth. Beaver pelts were the most common currency for Indigenous fur trappers and traders until the mid-nineteenth century, when point blankets replaced a decimated beaver population, and First Nations such as the Tsimshian and Haida used the two-point Hudson's Bay Company blanket as currency (Tichenor 15). "Rupert's Land" became part of Canada in 1870, three years after Confederation, and settlers used blankets, known as "annuity blankets," as a primary form of payment to First Nations peoples for title to their lands. The vexed colonial histories of the Hudson's Bay Company are often subsumed by nostalgia, collector cultures, and fashion's ongoing appreciation of the iconic blanket, but by projecting the animated scene, with blanket mid-air, *Witness* fulfills its title.

As a member of the Seneca nation—one of the six that makes up the Haudenosaunee (People of the Longhouse)—Watt honors her culture and inheritance by offering blankets back to the community. Seneca people (and other Native nations and communities) give away blankets to honor people for bearing witness to significant life events—a birth or death, graduations, naming ceremonies, a marriage. Watt opposes the psychoanalytic interpretation of blankets as transitional objects, but instead argues they are *transformational*:

Blankets are a part of how we are received into the world and also how we depart this world. Blankets are used for warmth and shelter. Children use them for hiding and to construct impromptu forts. A blanket is a catcher of dreams and ledger of secrets. Wool blankets are the pelts of our animal relatives, the sheep. Blankets are body-like.[7]

Blanket Stories: Western Door, Salt Sacks, Three Sisters (2017), a collaboration with the Rockwell Museum in Corning, New York, and the Corning community, features donated blankets from local residents of the greater Finger Lakes region and people associated with the Rockwell. Watt set up a call for blankets in September 2016; people were to donate a blanket along with a narrative or a memory associated with the blanket. If a person could not give up a blanket, they could still submit a narrative tag, which would be attached to a proxy blanket. All blankets were then shipped to Watt's studio in Portland, cleaned, tagged, and prepared for the sculpture. As with all of her blanket towers, twists, monoliths, and totems, the singular multiplied and replicated creates a sense of collectivity and community. Each memory carried and embodied by a blanket accrues toward a collective memory.

Western Door, Salt Sacks, Three Sisters rests atop an assemblage, a solid plinth, of oddly shaped stones that vary in size and tone, which Watt and others gathered from quarries near Corning. While they are reminiscent of a classic monument's base—granite, marble, cement, or brick—these stones are atomized, broken up. And yet together, they manage the weight of blankets and story. The *Blanket Stories* installations refuse to let viewers take the blanket for granted. As large-scale sculptures that sometimes twist and turn to form a kind of skyward bridge, the blankets overwhelm, spatially and affectively. When I begin to contemplate how each blanket carries a folded story, a memory—or sometimes

FIGURE 16 *Companion Species (Listening)* (2017) by Marie Watt.

many—the room suddenly feels crowded with ghosts, with Watt as their steward and guide.

"Listening is hard," Watt writes in response to her 2017 piece *Companion Species (Listening)*. It "requires continued work." On a reclaimed wool blanket (10.5 × 35.75 inches), two embroidered wolves face one another, each with one ear trained to the other wolf, and the other ear tuned to the space outside the field between them.

Watt's mother, Romayne Watt, says, "We have two ears and one mouth because the Creator intended us to listen twice as hard."[8] Marie Watt takes this knowledge seriously, her art an invitation, a generous offer, to tell a story, as when she wrote to me, "I wish I had asked you more about your brother and the blanket story you share."[9]

If blankets are monumental objects, carriers of story, and books contain stories, can a book be a monument, a rock? A ghost? I know books are made of sheets and covers. Can a book be a blanket too?

UNFOLD 7

I remember watching a nature show about foxes. It was a Sunday morning, but we weren't getting ready for mass. The priest would probably say a private mass at our house again. Did everyone but me know this was the day he would die?

The phrase *Kevin died*, or was it *Kevin just died*—the difference matters to me—hovered like the announcement of a friend's arrival, or the request to join the family at the dinner table. It was the kind of statement that quietly summoned action.

I kicked myself out from under the blanket, a frantic running-in-place motion while supine on the couch, all wrapped up to watch the foxes. As soon as I got to my feet, I set out to run to his room, but then I slowed myself down. There was no need to hurry now. My movements from the scene of projected foxes to the scene of Kevin, under his covers as always, but now dead, was a series of stop-motion contortions. If anyone had been watching, it would appear as if I were moving on my own. But some other force assembled the atoms that took me to his deathbed.

I wonder which one of us came back later to find the pile of two blankets—one mine, the other my sister's. I wonder if that person thought, *Who left this mess*? Or maybe, *The last time this kept a body warm on this late January day, Kevin was alive*. Someone folded those blankets.

I can't say what happened next that day. My crystalline memories of those hours after stay with me, and with the blankets and folds that carried his body away.

NOTES

Preface

1 World Health Organization, "Guide to Hygiene and Sanitation in Aviation," 3rd ed., 2009, 55–6. Nearly four billion people flew in 2016. "Another Strong Year for Air Travel Demand in 2016," International Air Transport Association, February 2, 2017, http://www.iata.org/pressroom/pr/Pages/2017-02-02-01.aspx.

2 Matt Phillips, "Airline Blankets: Nasty or Not?" *Wall Street Journal*, August 14, 2008, http://blogs.wsj.com/middleseat/2008/08/14/airplane-blankets-nasty-or-not/.

3 Catherine Sirna, "Delta launches exclusive Westin Heavenly In-Flight blanket for first class customers," October 26, 2016, http://news.delta.com/delta-launches-exclusive-westin-heavenly-flight-blanket-first-class-customers.

Chapter 1

1 Three weeks before Trayvon Martin was killed, and two years before Michael Brown and Eric Garner, 18-year-old Ramarley Graham was shot and killed by Officer Richard Haste. Graham was unarmed and standing in his own bathroom.

Haste's hollow-point bullet, which New York City police officers have used since the department switched from full metal jackets in the late 1990s, did what it was designed to do. Michael Cooper, "New York Police Will Start Using Deadlier Bullets," *New York Times*, July 9, 1998, http://www.nytimes.com/1998/07/09/nyregion/new-york-police-will-start-using-deadlier-bullets.html. James D. Walsh, "The Bullet, the Cop, the Boy," *New York*, June 14, 2017, http://nymag.com/daily/intelligencer/2017/06/ramarley-graham-nypd-shooting.html.

2   Medical practitioners and psychologists had struggled since at least the Civil War to theorize and diagnose soldiers and veterans, given the physical and psychological duress induced by combat. For instance, Dr. Jacob da Costa diagnosed Civil War soldiers' heart problems as "irritable heart." The term emphasized the physiological effects of marching, lack of sleep, and malnutrition. But da Costa reasoned that these were conditions of what he called "hard service," rather than effects of psychological trauma. Jacob M. da Costa, "On Irritable Heart: A Clinical Study of a Form of Functional Cardiac Disorder and Its Consequences," *American Journal of the Medical Sciences* 61, no. 121 (1871).

3   For instance, Sigmund Freud, *Charcot* (1893). Standard Edition, vol. 3 (London: The Hogarth Press, 1962); Freud, *Project for a Scientific Psychology*. Standard Edition, vol. 1 (London: The Hogarth Press, 1950); William James, *The Principles of Psychology* (Cambridge, MA: Harvard University Press, 1890); Jacques Dayan and Bertrand Olliac, "From Hysteria and Shell Shock to Posttraumatic Stress Disorder: Comments on Psychoanalytic and Neuropsychological Approaches," *Journal of Physiology-Paris* 104, no. 6 (2010): 296–302.

4 The term *shell shock* first appeared in *The Lancet* in 1915—
six months after the start of World War I —in an article by
an academic psychologist, Charles Myers, who had been
involved with a volunteer medical unit in France. Though
Myers was the first to introduce the term into medical
discourse, combat soldiers may have invented "shell shock"
to describe the physiological trauma associated with the
technologies of modern warfare. As Tracey Loughran argues,
the "act of naming was significant, not least because 'shell
shock' posited a shell explosion as the central etiological event
in these disorders." "Shell Shock, Trauma, and the First World
War: The Making of a Diagnosis and Its Histories," *Journal of
the History of Medicine and Allied Sciences* 67, no. 1 (2012):
94–119; 105. See also Charles Myers, "A Contribution to the
Study of Shell Shock: Being an Account of Three Cases of
Loss of Memory, Vision, Smell, and Taste, Admitted into the
Duchess of Westminster's War Hospital, Le Touquet," *Lancet*
1 (1915): 316–20; Caroline Alexander, "The Shock of War,"
The Smithsonian Magazine (September 2010), https://www.
smithsonianmag.com/history/the-shock-of-war-55376701/;
Marc-Antoine Crocq and Louis Crocq, "From Shell Shock
and War Neurosis to Posttraumatic Stress Disorder: A History
of Psychotraumatology," *Dialogues in Clinical Neuroscience* 2,
no. 1 (2000): 47–55; and Dayan and Olliac.

5 Anne Trafton, "Iron-plated snail could inspire new armor,"
MIT News (January 27, 2010), http://news.mit.edu/2010/
snail-shell.

6 Following Jane Bennett: "There is something to be said for
moments of methodological naïveté, for the postponement
of genealogical critique of objects. This delay might render
manifest a subsistent world of nonhuman vitality." *Vibrant
Matter*, 17.

7 To my knowledge, Parkman was the first historian to record the smallpox blanket strategy devised by Bouquet and Amherst during Pontiac's War.

8 See Parkman's note 1 on p. 40 about the provenance of Amherst's postscript. One of Amherst's letters was lost or destroyed, but the others from which Parkman cites were "among the manuscripts of the British Museum, *Bouquet and Haldimand Papers,* No. 21, 634."

9 Cited in Elizabeth A. Fenn, *Pox Americana: The Great Smallpox Epidemic of 1775–82* (New York: Hill and Wang, 2001); Philip Ranlet, "The British, the Indians, and Smallpox: What Actually Happened At Fort Pitt in 1763?" *Pennsylvania History: A Journal of Mid-Atlantic Studies* 67, no. 3 (2000): 427–41; and Bernhard Knollenberg, "General Amherst and Germ Warfare," *Mississippi Valley Historical Review* 41 (1954): 489–94. Knollenberg originally cited Trent in an attempt to exonerate Bouquet and Amherst, but later retracted after Donald Kent refuted Knollenberg's claims in 1955. See Kent and Knollenberg, "Communications," *Mississippi Valley Historical Review* 41, no. 4 (March 1955): 762–63 and Mayor, 58 and 72–3 note 5.

10 The precise numbers have been debated and disputed since at least the 1960s, but as Jeffrey Ostler puts it, "If 75 million people lived in the Western Hemisphere in 1491 and the death toll from epidemic disease was 70, 80, or even 90 percent (as was sometimes the case), the sheer numbers (50-60 million) are overwhelming and compel recognition as genocide when measured against the numbers for commonly accepted cases of genocide in the twentieth century." Even still, Ostler seems skeptical of the smallpox blanket, or at least notes that the "evidence thus far has failed to dislodge a scholarly consensus that the intentional infliction of disease was rare." See also Paul Kelton, *Epidemics and Enslavement: Biological Catastrophe in the Native Southeast, 1492–1715* (Lincoln: University of Nebraska Press, 2007).

11 Colin G. Calloway includes the "gifting" of smallpox blankets in his timeline on p. xvi of *The Scratch of a Pen: 1763 and the Transformation of North America* (Oxford: Oxford University Press, 2007). My summary of the Seven Years' War and Pontiac's War also come from this book.

12 The first known death related to HIV-AIDS was discovered in a sample of blood plasma from a man in Kinshasa in the Democratic Republic of Congo who died in 1959. The SIV, or Simian Immunodeficiency Virus, was likely something that the rand-capped mangabey and the greater spot-nosed guenon—two species of monkey—lived with for millions of years. But when chimpanzees started hunting these monkeys about eight million years ago, SIV likely jumped to chimpanzees, who were later hunted and butchered by humans. SIV and HIV are retroviruses, which means that the virus begins with the RNA code (instead of DNA), and then translates it into DNA before it transfers itself to the DNA of its host, where it proceeds with its life cycle.

13 Gerald M. Boyd, "Reagan Urges Abstinence for Young to Avoid AIDS," *New York Times,* April 2, 1987, http://www.nytimes.com/1987/04/02/us/reagan-urges-abstinence-for-young-to-avoid-aids.html.

14 Hal J. Cole, agent at the Colville Indian Agency in present-day Washington describes in his 1890 report: "The population is placed at 1,715 of which 300 is estimated; the number of actual names obtained is 1,415. The Indians are making progress in civilization; still the blanket Indian is more numerous than he should be. I found many more 'blanket' Indians here than I anticipated on coming to assume charge of the agency. . . ." The category of "Indian" was added to the census in 1860, but census takers were instructed only to include Native Americans whom they considered to be properly assimilated. The census did not attempt to count Native peoples officially until 1890, at which point enumerators typically used blood quantum to determine a person's proper category. For more, see: http://www.pewsocialtrends.org/2015/06/11/chapter-1-race-and-multiracial-americans-in-the-u-s-census/#fn-20523-23. The inclusion of Native Americans in the census demarcates a settler-colonial ideology that understands indigeneity as a racial and ethnic category, rather than Native peoples' status as tribal citizens of their nations.

15 I thank Jessica Cowing, not only for introducing me to this source, but for helping me understand the entangled discourses of health, ableism, civility, and heteronormativity in boarding schools.

16 And in 1879, Pratt sought and secured permission from the Secretary of the Interior and the Secretary of War to use the Carlisle Barracks—an Army installation established in 1745—as the site for the off-reservation boarding school. The former school is now a site for a military school, the US Army War College. For more on Fort Marion see Diane Glancy, *Fort Marion Prisoners and the Trauma of Native Education* (Lincoln: University of Nebraska Press, 2014); Donal F. Lindsey, *Indians at Hampton Institute, 1877–1923* (Urbana: University of Illinois Press, 1995), 27–33. For more on Pratt, Fort Marion, and the militarization of boarding schools see Brenda J. Child, *Boarding School Seasons: American Indian Families 1900–1940* (Lincoln: University of Nebraska Press, 1998), 5–6. And for more on Carlisle and Pratt see David

Wallace Adams, *Education for Extinction: American Indians and the Boarding School Experience, 1875–1928* (Lawrence: University Press of Kansas, 1995).

17 Hakiktawin's statement was made to E. Y. Berry, a Notary Public, in January 1934. See also David W. Grua, *Surviving Wounded Knee: The Lakotas and the Politics of Memory* (Oxford: Oxford University Press, 2016); and Julian Brave Noisecat and Anne Spice, "A History and Future of Resistance," *Jacobin* (2016): https://www.jacobinmag.com/2016/09/standing-rock-dakota-access-pipeline-protest/.

18 During Peltier's 1977 trial, an FBI ballistics expert testified that a casing found near the agents' body matched a gun that belonged to Peltier. However, the test that proved no connection between the casing and his gun was concealed and not introduced at the trial.

Chapter 2

1 After the 1932 Olympics, held in Los Angeles, the Public Works Administration sponsored a Master Tree Plan, and from 1933 to 1935, funds from the state gas tax covered tree maintenance on major streets and state highways. "The History of Urban Forestry Division," Bureau of Street Services and Department of Public Works for the City of Los Angeles, 2017, http://bss.lacity.org/urbanforestry/History.htm.

2 The Indian fig, or ficus, takes only thirty to forty years to grow above the roofline of an average ranch house. The California live oak, a native species, takes much longer to grow, and so city developers went with ficus.

3   *Stripe Hand Towel* (2011) makes a similar argument: With
    acrylic paint, Saban creates an uncanny hand towel that
    covers a 20 × 16 × 1 ¼-inch canvas. Three edges of the canvas
    are visible, again, just enough to evoke the conventional
    relation of canvas to paint.

4   *Analia Saban: The Whole Ball of Wax* (New York: Gregory
    R. Miller & Co., 2017), 14.

5   Some of the cuts in the Calacata Borghini quarry date back
    to the Roman Empire. M. Pilar Lapuente, Bruno Turi, and
    Philippe Blanc, "Marbles From Roman Hispania: Stable
    Isotope and Cathodoluminescence Characterization," *Applied
    Geochemistry* 15, no. 10 (2000): 1469–93.

6   Interview with the author, July 26, 2017.

7   To visit the marble mines in the Apuan Alps, visitors must hire
    guides or take a private jeep tour, and the yet the material is made
    perversely available and accessible for home renovation.

8   A highly adaptable material, concrete is an aggregate of
    broken stone or gravel mixed with sand, cement, and water.
    Ancient Romans mixed pozzuolana (volcanic earth) with
    lime, broken stones, and tuff to create concrete for roads and
    large buildings; cement was not a component of concrete until
    the mid-nineteenth century. See "Concrete," in *The Columbia
    Encyclopedia* (New York: Columbia University Press, 2017).

9   "Marble in Afghanistan," a brochure available from Afghanistan's
    Ministry of Mining, describes an industry that "suffers from a
    lack of adequate equipment, has little technical knowledge, and
    uses poor extraction methods that often significantly reduce
    the value of the marble." The marble is extracted from twelve
    different provinces, then exported to Pakistan in rough-hewn
    blocks to be proceeded, then transported back to Afghanistan.
    An updated version of the brochure concludes with a call to

private and foreign investors to help "develop the huge and very diverse mineral resource potential of Afghanistan." Ministry of Mines and Petroleum and United States Agency of International Development (USAID), January 16, 2014.

10 I've simplified Deleuze's metaphor somewhat, since he folds yet another analogy into marble, "*like an undulating lake full of fish*" (229).

11 I think of this somewhat like Carlo Rovelli's description of space as matter: "We are not contained within an invisible, rigid infrastructure: we are immersed in a gigantic, flexible snail shell. The sun bends space around itself, and Earth does not turn around it because of a mysterious force but because it is racing directly in a space that inclines, like a marble that rolls in a funnel." Carlo Rovelli, *Seven Brief Lessons on Physics* (New York: Riverhead Books, 2016), 8.

Chapter 3

1 "Navajo Ute First Phase Blanket, ca. 1850," Antiques Roadshow, video, 3:48, accessed July 2017, http://www.pbs.org/wgbh/roadshow/season/6/tucson-az/appraisals/navajo-first-phase-blanket--200101A48/.

2 See also Donna Haraway, *Staying With the Trouble: Making Kin in the Chthulucene* (Durham, NC: Duke University Press, 2016), 89–97.

3 *Dah iisłʼó Bizaad* was installed in the *Hear My Voice: Native American Art of the Past and Present* exhibition at the Virginia Museum of Fine Arts (Richmond, VA: August 19, 2017–November 26, 2017). The quotes by Begay here accompany her blanket.

4   "eyeDazzler," dir. by Will Wilson and Dylan McLaughlin, 2012, video, 2:51, https://vimeo.com/34320606.

5   With Josh Sarantitis and Greg Barton, Wilson developed open-source software, TilePile, which converts pixels into the color palette for glass tiles. They originally developed TilePile for the Barrio Anita Mural Project in Tucson, AZ.

6   "Diabetes Burden Strap, DNA Mircroarray Analysis," 2008, http://ericalord.com/artwork/897025-Diabetes-Burden-Strap-DNA-Mircroarray-Analysis.html.

7   "My First Baby Belt," 2007, http://ericalord.com/artwork/167190-My-First-Baby-Belt.html.

8   According to the Indian Health Service (IHS), Native/Indigenous people "have the highest rates of type 2 diabetes in the United States." "Special Diabetes Program for Indians," Indian Health Service, October 2016, https://www.ihs.gov/newsroom/factsheets/diabetes/. IHS reports that the prevalence of diabetes (type 1 or 2 is not specified) in Native/Indigenous people in 2012 was 35 percent for those 65 and older, between 20 and 25 percent for those 45 to 64, 5 percent for those 20 to 44, and between 0 and 5 percent for those under 20. "Changing the Course of Diabetes: Turning Hope into Reality," Indian Health Service, Special Diabetes Program for Indians, 2014 Report to Congress, https://www.ihs.gov/newsroom/reportstocongress/, 2.

9   Colleen Kim Daniher also reads this piece as a critique of blood quantum and DNA tests that attempt to quantify one's genetic inheritance. This argument certainly links up with Lord's body of work, which critiques, enlivens, and grapples with the experience of living with a mixed cultural identity, moving between disparate spaces, and always existing "somewhere in between" in terms of her notion of home and culture. See "The Pose as Interventionist Gesture: Erica

Lord and Decolonizing the Proper Subject of Memory," *Hemispheric Institute E-Misphérica* 11, no. 1 (2014), http://hemisphericinstitute.org/hemi/en/emisferica-111-decolonial-gesture/daniher and http://ericalord.com/home.html.

10 In an interview with Arizona Public Media in 2016, Kuntz mentions that his grandmother "had grown up with" Mark Bedell, and the "story goes that Kit Carson gave this blanket to Mark Bedell." "The Navajo Blanket," *Arizona Public Media* (June 21, 2016): https://tv.azpm.org/p/originals-azill-arts/2016/6/21/90434-the-navajo-blanket/.

11 The quote about Bedell's hide post comes from John M. Motter, "Did Army Make Dutch Henry an Outlaw?" *Pagosa Springs Sun* (September 19, 2002). For more on the eliminatory and acquisitive strategies of settlers see Patrick Wolfe, "Settler Colonialism and the Elimination of the Native," *Journal of Genocide Research* 8, no. 4 (2006): 387–409; and Nicholas A. Brown, "The Logic of Settler Accumulation in a Landscape of Perpetual Vanishing," *Settler Colonial Studies* 4, no. 1 (2014): 1–26.

12 Kuntz sold the blanket to an anonymous buyer who then donated it to the Detroit Institute of Arts.

13 Personal correspondence with the author, January 2018.

14 Connie Butler, "Jeanine Oleson: Conduct Matters," *Hammer Project* (Los Angeles: May 2017). Exhibition brochure.

15 Quoted in Alex Teplitzky, "Jeanine Oleson's Critique of Capitalism Through Craft and Humor," *Creative Capital*, May 25, 2017, http://blog.creative-capital.org/2017/05/jeanine-olesons-critique-capitalism-craft-humor/.

16 "Duck and Cover" by Archer Productions (1951) available at https://archive.org/details/DuckandC1951.

Chapter 4

1   "Food or blankets?" *The Lancet* 341, no. 8857 (May 29, 1993): 1407.

2   Morrigan McCarthy, "Harvey in Pictures," *New York Times*, August 27, 2017, https://www.nytimes.com/2017/08/27/us/harvey-pictures-hurricane-storm.html. The specific photo I refer to is by Edmund D. Fountain.

3   Emily Crockett, "It could take years for Texas abortion clinics to reopen, even after a Supreme Court victory," *Vox*, June 27, 2016, https://www.vox.com/2016/6/27/12038934/supreme-court-texas-whole-womans-health-closed-clinics-reopen-years.

4   Texas senator John Cornyn released the following statement after the ruling: "Today 5 activist judges on the Supreme Court struck down key provisions of Texas' pro-life omnibus bill. This law not only protected unborn life, but required that doctors be qualified when providing life threatening procedures and that these procedures be done in a safe environment." "Texas Republicans Slam Supreme Courts' HB2 Ruling," June 27, 2016, accessed September 2017, http://kfyo.com/reaction-texas-hb2-supreme-court-ruling/.

5   Ginsburg, J., concurring, *Whole Woman's Health, et al., Petitioners v. John Hellerstedt, Commissioner, Texas Department of State Health Services, et al.*, 579 U.S. 2 (2016). See also Mark Joseph Stern, "Supreme Court Strikes Down Texas Abortion Restrictions," *Slate,* June 27, 2016, http://www.slate.com/blogs/the_slatest/2016/06/27/supreme_court_strikes_down_texas_abortion_law_hb2.html.

6   This chapter offers an extensive reading of Sherman Alexie's story "War Dances." *Blanket* was already well into production when allegations of Alexie's sexual harassment were made public in March 2018.

7   "The Thomas Kay Collection: A Pioneer's Legacy," March 2013: https://blog.pendleton-usa.com/2013/03/01/the-thomas-kay-collection-a-pioneers-legacy/. See History of the Confederated Tribes of the Umatilla Indian Reservation for an overview of the history that leads to the settler nation forcing tribes onto the reservation in the early 1860s: http://ctuir.org/history-culture/history-ctuir. For an in-depth study and history of this region and its Native peoples, see Andrew H. Fisher, *Shadow Tribe: The Making of Columbia River Indian Identity* (Seattle: University of Washington Press, 2010).

8   https://www.pendleton-usa.com/our-community.html.

9   Conversation with George Ciscle, December 15, 2017. Ciscle, former director of the MFA in Curatorial Practice at the Maryland Institute College of Art (MICA), curated the first exhibition of Elizabeth Talford Scott's lifelong work in 1998. Ciscle also conducted extensive oral interviews with Scott, and these comprise a rich and invaluable archive of her life and work. All references and attributions cited in *Blanket* come from Ciscle's interviews and the exhibition catalogue.

10 In the genealogy of Black Codes and convict leasing, chain gangs were another post-abolition method to criminalize and incarcerate African Americans. Georgia was the first state to institute chain gangs to force male convicts into arduous labor—chains were wrapped around their ankles, and men were shackled to fellow prisoners while they worked, ate, and slept. Chain gangs were abolished in the 1950s, but as recently as 1995, the Staton and Limestone correctional facilities in Alabama reinstituted chain gangs.

11 "Humane Restraint HSB-100 Suicide Safety Blanket," American Detention Supplies, 2017, https://www.americandetentionsupplies.com/safety-restraints/suicide-smocks-blankets/humane-restraint-suicide-safety-blanket-detail.

12 Project Linus, http://www.projectlinus.org.

13 https://everytownresearch.org/school-shootings/.

14 Dyneema®, https://www.dsm.com/products/dyneema/en_US/home.html.

15 "Dyneema® in Personal Armor," https://www.dsm.com/products/dyneema/en_US/applications/personal-armor.html. Dyneema's slogan: "We're with you when it matters."

16 Interview with Catherine Sweeney from *NewsOK*, "Oklahomans develop blanket to protect youngsters in tornadoes or shootings," June 7, 2014, accessed June 2017, http://newsok.com/oklahomans-develop-blanket-to-protect-youngsters-in-tornadoes-or-shootings/article/4888703.

17 Interview with Catherine Sweeney.

18 https://www.youtube.com/watch?v=iaS-ekAwwM4.

19 Greg Abbott (@GregAbbott_TX), Twitter, October 28, 2015, https://twitter.com/GregAbbott_TX/status/659427797853536256.

20 Tessa Stuart, "2015: The Year in Mass Shootings," *Rolling Stone* (December 3, 2015): https://www.rollingstone.com/politics/news/2015-the-year-in-mass-shootings-20151203.

21 Photo by Spencer Platt/Getty Images.

Chapter 5

1 In *Poetics*, Aristotle states: "Liveliness is especially conveyed by metaphor, and by the further power of surprising the hearer; because the hearer expected something different, his acquisition of the new idea impresses him all the more" (1412a, 18–24).

2 Throughout, I use the term *Oceti Sakowin* to refer to people of the Seven Council Fires—in dominant/settler discourse, the "Sioux" and "Great Sioux Nation." The Council Fires—formed according to kinship, language, and geographic proximity—are: Mdewakanton, Wahpekute, Sisitonwan/Sisseton, Wahpetonwan, Ihnaktown/Lower Yanktonai, Ihanktowana/Upper Yanktonai, and Tetonwan. There are seven bands of the Tetonwan/Teton, or *people of the plains*: Hunkpapa, Sicangu/Brule, Itazipo/Sans Arc, Sihasapa, Oglala, Oohenumpa, and Mniconjou. *Oyate* refers to *people*—the communities and bands that comprise the *Oceti Sakowin*.

3 For a smart and historicized take on the alliances between farmers/ranchers and Native nations (beyond the "Cowboys and Indians" discourse in the mainstream press), see Zoltán Grossman, *Unlikely Alliances: Native Nations and White Communities Join to Defend Rural Lands* (Seattle: University of Washington Press, 2017).

4 The full text is available at the Indigenous Environmental Network: http://www.ienearth.org/mother-earth-accord/.

5 http://www.ienearth.org/president-obama-rejects-keystone-xl-indigenous-environmental-network-responds/.

6 See maps created by Jennifer Veilleux and her team, posted on *High Country News* (November 5, 2016): http://www.hcn.org/articles/these-maps-fill-the-gap-in-information-about-the-dakota-access-pipeline.

7 Iŋyaŋ Wakháŋagapi Othí or Sacred Stone is the pre-colonial term for Cannon Ball in present-day North Dakota on the reservation lands of the Standing Rock Sioux Nation.

8 Permit 12, available at http://www.usace.army.mil/Portals/2/docs/civilworks/nwp/2012/NWP_12_2012.pdf.

9 http://lampherestudio.com/dignity/.

10 Late eighteenth- to nineteenth-century Hudson's Bay
Company blankets were typically red, blue, or white—all with
black bars—but according to Harold Tichenor, Kwakiutl and
Nuu-Cha-Nuth peoples (along the west coast of Canada)
"favored green blankets" (40).

11 The Plymouth Historical Museum in Michigan installed an
exhibition for over five years, "Quilts of the Underground
Railroad," which presented the thesis from *Hidden in Plain
View.* "Unraveling the Myth of Quilts and the Underground
Railroad," *Time* (April 3, 2007): http://content.time.com/time/
arts/article/0,8599,1606271,00.html.

12 Tobin narrates her first encounter with Williams, and later
a telephone call in which Williams told her "Don't worry,
you'll get the story when you're ready" and then hung up.
Tobin didn't speak to Williams again for three years when she
found her in the same market and Williams began to relay the
details of the code system. See pp. 15–23.

13 Giles R. Wright's written statement may be accessed at http://
historiccamdencounty.com/ccnews11_doc_01a.shtml. This is
a truncated portion of this keynote address—a more detailed
critique of *Hidden in Plain View*—from June 4, 2001, at the
Underground Railroad Day at the Camden County Historical
Society. Wright died in 2009.

14 "Unraveling the Myth of Quilts and the Underground
Railroad."

15 Given this chapter's focus, my own commitments and
knowledge-base, and the accelerations and propulsions
of *Blanket* more generally, I must leave an in-depth
engagement with the rich histories and ongoing practices
of African American quilting to others—especially to those
whose memories and forms of inheritance belong to the

legacies of this extraordinary practice. My understanding and knowledge have been instrumentally shaped by contemporary quilters like Dr. Joan M. E. Gaither and Dr. Riché Richardson; and their work deserves its own scholarly treatment. I want to thank Professor Richardson, especially, for inviting me to her studio in 2005–06 to view some of her exquisite quilts, and for teaching me, both in and outside the classroom, about quilts as collective memory, as forms of embodiment. Images of her work are available at http://richerichardsonartquilts.blogspot.com. For engaged studies of African American quilters and quilts, see Patricia A. Turner, *Crafted Lives: Stories and Studies of African American Quilters* (Jackson: University Press of Mississippi, 2009); William Arnett et al., *The Quilts of Gee's Bend* (Tinwood Books, 2002); Carolyn Mazloomi, *Spirits of the Cloth: Contemporary African American Quilts* (Clarkson Potter, 1998); Gladys-Marie Fry's *Stitched from the Soul: Slave Quilts from the Antebellum South* (Chapel Hill: University of North Carolina Press, 1990) and a special issue in the journal *Interdisciplinary Humanities* devoted to African American quilts and quiltmaking, 25, no. 2 (Fall 2008).

16 Miller characterizes the quilt code as perhaps "the first language in the New World, this geometric language of patterns," which gravely overlooks the innumerable languages of Native/Indigenous peoples spoken and signified in rock, textiles, hides, on pottery, and other materials for thousands of years on Turtle Island. This is an especially unfortunate oversight given that Miller himself notes that Frederick Douglass Circle is a counternarrative to (Christopher) Columbus Circle in Manhattan. His statement is available at http://www.slaveryinnewyork.org.

17 http://www.nytimes.com/learning/teachers/featured_
articles/20070124wednesday.html. Blight's books include:
*Passages to Freedom: The Underground Railroad in History
and Memory* (New York: Harper Collins, 2004). And his book
about Douglass, *Frederick Douglass' Civil War: Keeping Faith in
Jubilee* (Baton Rouge: Louisiana State University Press, 1989).

18 http://www.nyc.gov/html/dcla/html/panyc/miller.shtml.

19 *"Live Free or Die"* is in the Reginald F. Lewis Museum of
African American History & Culture (Baltimore, Maryland)
collections.

Chapter 6

1 The first iteration of *Blanket Stories* was installed at the
National Museum of the American Indian in late 2004.

2 http://www.mariewattstudio.com/projects/western-door.

3 http://www.oregonlive.com/art/index.ssf/2007/04/marie_watt_
blanket_stories.html.

4 http://blanketstories.tacomaartmuseum.org.

5 Photo archived at the Royal British Columbia Museum and
Archives. Marie Watt includes the photo below the image of
Witness here: http://www.mariewattstudio.com/work/project/
witness-2015.

6 Though the Company was not the first to introduce the wool
point blanket, it formally adopted it in 1780.

7 http://gregkucera.com/watt_earlier.htm.

8 http://www.mariewattstudio.com/work/project/companion-
species-listening-2017.

9 Artist correspondence with the author, August 12, 2017.

ACKNOWLEDGMENTS

My abiding gratitude to:

Haaris Naqvi, Ian Bogost, and Christopher Schaberg for this series, and to CS especially—Emerson was the crucial opening; the fabulous Jessica Cowing for citation sleuthing and the right questions; George Ciscle for *Rocks in Prison*, curation, and archives; Jeanine Oleson, Dario Robleto, and Will Wilson, whose work has shaped my thinking; Analia Saban and Marie Watt, who opened their studios to me; AS, your marble and concrete gave me permission; MW, your blankets guided me through; Carrie Brownstein for space and uneven sidewalks; Elizabeth Barnes, for grief and friendship; Dr. Paula Jean, for narratives and language; Chelsey Johnson, for all the reading and love; Brian and Tammy, for security and memory; and my parents, the bravest and tenderest people I know.

BIBLIOGRAPHY

Acheson, Donald. "Conflict in Bosnia 1992–3." *BMJ: British Medical Journal* 319, no. 7225 (December 1999): 1639–42.

Alexie, Sherman. "War Dances." In *War Dances*, 27–63. New York: Grove Press, 2009.

Anderson, Sam, and Luca Locatelli. "The Majestic Marble Quarries of Northern Italy." *New York Times Magazine* (July 26, 2017).

Bates, Robert L., and Julia A. Jackson, eds. *Dictionary of Geological Terms*. New York: Anchor Books, 1984.

Benjamin, Walter. "Excavation and Memory." In *Selected Writings* vol. 2, 1927–34, edited by Michael W. Jennings, Howard Eiland, and Gary Smith, 576. Cambridge, MA: Belknap Press, 1999.

Bennett, Jane. *Vibrant Matter: A Political Ecology of Things*. Durham, NC: Duke University Press, 2010.

Brown, Dee. *Bury My Heart at Wounded Knee: An Indian History of the American West*. New York: Sterling Signature, 2012.

Bsumek, Erika. *Indian-Made: Navajo Culture in the Marketplace, 1868–1940*. Lawrence: University Press of Kansas, 2008.

Ciscle, George, ed. *Eyewinkers, Tumbleturds and Candlebugs: The Art of Elizabeth Talford Scott*. Baltimore: Maryland Institute College of Art, 1998. Exhibition catalogue.

Cvetkovitch, Ann. "Trauma and Touch." In *An Archive of Feelings: Trauma, Sexuality, and Lesbian Public Cultures*. Durham, NC: Duke University Press, 2003.

Danticat, Edwidge. *The Art of Death: Writing the Final Story*, 29. Minneapolis, MN: Graywolf Press, 2017.

Dean, Tim. *Unlimited Intimacy: Reflections on the Subculture of Barebacking*. Chicago: University of Chicago Press, 2009.

Deleuze, Gilles. *The Fold: Leibniz and the Baroque*. Translated by Tom Conley. Minneapolis: University of Minnesota Press, 1993.

Deleuze, Gilles, and Jonathan Strauss. "The Fold." *Yale French Studies* 80 (1991): 227–47.

Estes, Nick. "Fighting for Our Lives: #NoDAPL in Historical Context." *The Red Nation* (September 2016): https://therednation.org.

Estes, Nick. "Wounded Knee: Settler Colonial Property Regimes and Indigenous Liberation." *Capitalism Nature Socialism* 24, no. 3 (2013): 190–202.

Freud, Sigmund. *Beyond the Pleasure Principle*. Translated by James Strachey. New York: W. W. Norton, 1961.

Herz, Norman, and David B. Wenner. "Tracing the Origins of Marble." *Archaeology* 34, no. 5 (1981): 14–21.

"Imprisoned." *The Youth's Companion* 70, no. 35 (August 27, 1896): 434.

Keene, Adrienne. "Let's Talk About Pendleton." *Native Appropriations* (February 3, 2011): http://nativeappropriations.com.

Kte'pi, Bill. "Potlatch." In *Multicultural America: A Multimedia Encyclopedia*, edited by Carlos E. Cortes, 1741–42. Thousand Oaks, CA: Sage Publications, 2013.

Leibniz, G. W. *Principles of Nature and Grace* (1714). In *Leibniz: Philosophical Essays*, edited by and translated by Roger Ariew and Daniel Garber, 206–13. Indianapolis and Cambridge: Hackett Publishing Company, 1989.

Long Soldier, Layli. "Vaporative." In *Whereas*, 23–27. Minneapolis: University of Minnesota Press, 2017.

Low, John N. *Imprints: The Pokagon Band of Potawatomi Indians and the City of Chicago*. East Lansing: Michigan State University Press, 2016.

Mannix, Rebekah. "The Blanket." *Annals of Emergency Medicine* 63, no. 3 (2015): 336.

Mayor, Adrienne. "The Nessus Shirt in the New World: Smallpox Blankets in History and Legend." *Journal of American Folklore* 108, no. 427 (1995): 54–77.

Mbiti, John. *African Religions and Philosophy*. Portsmouth, NH: Heinemann, 1990.

McGregor, James Herman. *The Wounded Knee Massacre from the Viewpoint of the Sioux*. Rapid City, SD: Fenske Printing Inc., 1940.

Ostler, Jeffrey. "Genocide and American Indian History." *Oxford Research Encyclopedia: American History* (March 2015).

Parkman, Francis. *The Conspiracy of Pontiac and the Indian War after the Conquest of Canada: From the Spring of 1763 to the Death of Pontiac* 2 (1851). Lincoln: University of Nebraska Press, 1994.

Peltier, Leonard. *Prison Writings: My Life is My Sun Dance*. Edited by Harvey Arden. New York: St. Martin's Press, 1999.

Pendleton Woolen Mills (1915). *Reprinted*. Albuquerque, NM: Avanyu Publishing, 1987.

Peterson, Richard. "Star Power: Piecing Together Tradition and Community." *Tribal College* 25, no. 1 (2013): 24–27.

Pratt, Richard Henry. *Battlefield & Classroom: Four Decades with the American Indian, 1867–1904* (1964). Edited by Robert M. Utley, Foreword by David Wallace Adams. Norman, OK: University of Oklahoma Press, 2003.

Reel, Estelle. *The Uniform Course of Study for the Indian Schools of the United States*. Washington, DC: Government Printing Office, 1901, 154.

Ritvo, Max. *Four Reincarnations*. Minneapolis, MN: Milkweed Editions, 2016.

Roach, Joseph. *Cities of the Dead: Circum-Atlantic Performance*. New York: Columbia University Press, 1996.

Rosen, Hannah. Personal communication with author, July 18, 2017.

Silko, Leslie Marmon. *Ceremony* (30th anniversary ed.). New York: Penguin, 2006.

Standing Bear, Luther. *Land of the Spotted Eagle* (1933). Lincoln, NE: Bison Books, 2006.

Stockton, Kathryn Bond. *The Queer Child, or Growing Sideways in the Twentieth Century*. Durham, NC: Duke University Press, 2009.

Tichenor, Harold. *The Blanket: An Illustrated History of the Hudson's Bay Point Blanket*. Toronto: Madison Press Books, 2002.

Tisdale, Shelby Jo-Anne, ed. *Spider Woman's Gift: Nineteenth-Century Diné Textiles at the Museum of Indian Arts and Culture*. Santa Fe: Museum of New Mexico Press, 2011.

Tobin, Jacqueline L., and Raymond G. Dobard. *Hidden in Plain View: A Secret Story of Quilts and the Underground Railroad*. New York: Anchor Books, 2000.

Voyles, Traci Brynne. *Wastelanding: Legacies of Uranium Mining in Navajo Country*. Minneapolis: University of Minnesota Press, 2015.

Watt, Marie. *Lodge*. Hallie Ford Museum of Art at Willamette University, February 4–April 1, 2012. Seattle: University of Washington Press, 2012. Exhibition catalogue.

Willink, Roseann Sandoval, and Paul G. Zolbrod. *Weaving a World: Textiles and the Navajo Way of Seeing*. Santa Fe: University of New Mexico Press, 1996.

Winnicott, D. W. *Playing and Reality* (1971). London: Routledge, 2005.

Zitkala-Sa. "The School Days of an Indian Girl." In *American Indian Stories, Legends, and Other Writings*, edited by Cathy Davidson and Ada Norris, 87–89. New York: Penguin Classics, 2003.

LIST OF FIGURES

INDEX

Page references for illustrations appear in *italics*.